Anonymous

The Psalter, or, Selections from the Book of Psalms

With other poetical Sriptures, for responsive reading in public worship

Anonymous

The Psalter, or, Selections from the Book of Psalms
With other poetical Sriptures, for responsive reading in public worship

ISBN/EAN: 9783337285982

Printed in Europe, USA, Canada, Australia, Japan

Cover: Foto ©Lupo / pixelio.de

More available books at **www.hansebooks.com**

# The Psalter;

OR,

SELECTIONS FROM

The Book of Psalms:

WITH OTHER POETICAL SCRIPTURES,

FOR RESPONSIVE READING IN

PUBLIC WORSHIP.

A. S. BARNES & COMPANY,
NEW YORK AND CHICAGO.

Copyright, 1883, *by* A. S. BARNES & CO

PREFACE.

NEARLY twenty years ago the church, of which the writer was and still is the Pastor, adopted the responsive reading of the Psalms, by the Minister and the Congregation, at each Service on the Lord's Day, as a prescribed and permanent part of its public worship.

As it was the wish of all there concerned with the matter to have the ancient hymns read antiphonally, dividing the successive verses into their parallel and responding clauses, and as no book was then at hand in which they were suitably printed for this purpose, or were arranged in 'Lessons' of a convenient length, a small volume was hastily prepared, which it was thought might for a time supply the need of the waiting congregation.

It has served its purpose well, and has silently made its way, to the grateful surprise of the compiler, into more than four hundred churches, of different communions, in our own country, and into American chapels in Europe.

The custom of such responsive reading has also secured earnest friends, and enlisted for itself their intelligent interest, wherever it has been tried; and while, at the outset, a not unreasonable fear was entertained, by those to whom the thought of it was new, that it might tend to protract unduly the services of worship, or possibly to introduce into such services an element of 'formalism,' of questionable value, so far as is known the congregations which have adopted it would now be entirely unwilling to displace it. Their attachment to it grows, as the custom continues.

It is believed to have proved itself, beyond the expectation of those who first favored it, a useful and a delightful part of public worship:—instructive, by continually recalling the minds of congregations to the jubilant or pathetic words of the Scripture, in which experience has given a voice to the teachings of revelation; inspiring to devotion, by the quickening impression which it communicates of that intense, ever-living temper, of adoration, trust, penitence, hope, which has never found another expression so majestic or so tender as in these ancient consecrated lyrics; exalting to the tone of worship—illuminating, even, as to the intrinsic nobleness of its function—since it unites, in spirit certainly, and measurably in form, the worship of to-day, in recent congregations, with that of the day of martyrs and confessors, whose most familiar and hallowed songs were the Psalms, responsively chanted; with that of the synagogue, in which the Master was wont to worship; with that, indeed, of the august Temple, divinely appointed, by whose educating services the way of the Lord was prepared on the earth, and all whose types shall find their only complete fulfilment in the day of the glory of the Church Universal.

The objection to prescribed forms of prayer, of human composition—though framed by men as properly revered as Calvin or Melancthon, as Chrysostom or Basil—is one which will probably always continue widely to be felt. Multitudes of Christians will certainly prefer, hereafter as now, that the Minister shall offer the public confession, supplication, and thanksgiving, as he did in the day of Justin Martyr, even at the solemn celebration of the Eucharist, "according to his ability"; that this shall be to him a motive for intent and prayerful preceding preparation for the service of God's House; and that on his worshipping spirit, as moved from above to immediate utterance of desire and praise, the spirit of the assembly shall be uplifted toward the Throne in the Heavens.

But no theory of church-worship can be sustained, no practice of it will remain satisfactory, which does not provide a large place for the reading of the Scriptures; and no form of Divine Service will ever accomplish its best effects for those who take part in it which does not engage the interested attention alike of the older and the younger, by calling on all to perform in it fitting and solemn responsive offices. Dumbness, when voluntary, seems related to stupor. The Church which strives, and is victorious, spontaneously seeks acclaiming voices, as well as the notes of trumpet and organ, to animate the struggle, and to celebrate the joy.

The recital of the Psalms, on every Lord's Day, by the Minister and the People answering each other, appears wholly free from just objection. It not only assures, as has been suggested, important direct aids and benefits to those engaged in it; it has the delightful charm upon it of demonstrating freshly, all the time, the perennial unity of feeling and of faith, among those who bear different Christian names, but who equally turn to the venerated Psalter for instruction and impulse in the things of experience: who are almost ready, even, to say of it, as many devout singers of the Church have reverently said, "all my springs are in thee." It seems as certain as any thing in the future that this is to be, more and more, a familiar and a favorite practice with congregations which delight in the prayers of the Psalms, not less than in their praises, though nowise inclined to accept the use of liturgical forms. The 'Songs of degrees' have been named, rather, by a distinguished critical scholar, 'Songs of the homeward marches.' All the Psalms have been felt to be such by many devout and faithful spirits, as they have sung them in the paths of their pilgrimage, towards the Home upon the heavenly hills. The Church itself is more and more to find them such, as it advances toward Millennium.

In connection with the lessons of encouragement and of counsel which have

PREFACE.

come from many years' use of the Psalms, in the manner referred to, the need of a book adapted to the purpose, more complete than the one first compiled, and more carefully arranged, has for some time been recognized; and the present volume is the fruit of a wish to supply such need, at least for one beloved congregation.

The Psalms contained in it are divided as before, according to the rule of that intrinsic and governing 'Thought-rhythm' which constitutes a characteristic beauty of Hebrew poetry; and they are arranged, as far as possible, with reference to their principal subjects, and their prevalent tone of feeling, without regard to the order of the pages on which they have been wont to be printed, or to the possible or probable order of the dates of their composition. The end in view being the present practical impressiveness of this part of worship, and its rich fruitfulness in spiritual impulse, an inward unity has been sought in the selections; and external questions, concerning them or their authors, have been wholly laid aside. A Psalm of supplication is thus associated with others of its kind; while those of adoration, confidence, hope, are similarly combined.

This seems the most appropriate way of using the ancient and quickening lyrics, in a modern assembly, and the way most truly honorable to them. Whatever differences of historical relation appear in different parts of the Psalter, the whole constitutes, plainly, a realm by itself, in the imperial compass of the Scripture; as much so as does the earlier Pentateuch, whose division into five books, the somewhat similar traditional division of the Psalter into five associated parts has often been said to resemble. The whole collection of petitions and praises grew out of the unique career of the People of God, from the day of Moses, the Servant of God, down toward if not to the day of the Maccabees. It is equally available, in all its extent, to those who would use it for present ministration to spiritual feeling. And it is obviously wholly unimportant, with reference to this office, whether two Psalms were composed or not by the same writer, were composed or not at about the same time; whether they sprang out of one set of circumstances, or out of two, resembling each other, though separated by years; whether they have been commonly printed side by side, or on different leaves, in the copies of the Bible. As hymns born of the Holy Ghost, when touching with divinest fire the souls of their respective writers, they are properly associated, in a volume like this, by the essential harmonies which they show in their present appeal to the mind of the worshipper. Any other possible order of arrangement, for the purpose in view, must of necessity be mechanical and confusing. The compiler is quite aware that he has not always accomplished his purpose. The difficulties in the way of a perfect success will present themselves at once to any who follow him in his endeavor. But his rule has been, that only by their special coincidences of sentiment and tone are the hymns, whose common inspiration he rejoices to recognize, fitly connected with each other in a manual like the present.

PREFACE.

In deference to a wish expressed by others, rather than from any strong impulse in himself, he has added to the collection of Psalms some other selections, not only from Messianic prophecies, but from the poetry of the book of Job, from the Proverbs, from Ecclesiastes, and one or two from the book of The Revelation. It has been thought that such passages—especially those which represent the gnomic and didactic poetry of the ancient church, widely differing in tone from the lyric, though kindred in structure—may be found to be of use, particularly on occasion of exceptional services.

It is hoped that the book, as now arranged, may prove acceptable to those who have come to prize and to love that element in worship which it would subserve, but who have felt the obvious deficiencies of the preceding collection. It is hoped, also, that it may tend, in the measure of its influence, to commend the responsive reading of the Psalms to still other congregations, who may wish to expand and enrich their services, making them at once more popular in their character, and also more serious, more scriptural, more devout.

But whether it shall have a wide circulation, or one more restricted, it has brought already its rich reward to him who has arranged it. It has led him into contact, day by day, while he has been occupied in the work of preparing it, with the devout and heroical spirits of the past ; from whom our arts and sciences were hid, and who had not the full vision of Christ, but who alone, in the world of their time, saw God in His glory, and expected the triumph of His kingdom in the earth ; who were penetrated profoundly with the sense of their sinfulness, but who were at the same time exultingly aware of the power and grace which remained for them in the heavens ; who were therefore courageous in the midst of adversity, and humble and grateful in the day of success; whose prayers have always praises in them, while the most joyful melodies of their worship are full, as well, of supplication ; through whom the Spirit divinely spake.

His self-imposed task has thus brought to the writer a constantly fresh and clearer sense of the spiritual riches infolded with a skill surpassing man's in this book of the Scriptures, which has been well named 'the Little Bible.' And whatever of time and of thought have been called for, in the work of arranging them for wider use among the churches, are gratefully dedicated to Him whom the Psalms invoke and celebrate, with an utterance rivalling the reach of the heavens in sovereign sublimity, yet fitting itself to the varying needs of worshipping souls with an adjustment as distinct as that of the sunshine to human eyes :—and to those, as well, by whatever name distinguished among men, who love and who seek His earthly courts !

R. S. STORRS.

BROOKLYN, N. Y., *March* 17, 1883.

The Ten Commandments.

[Exodus XX : 1—17.]

AND God spake all these words, saying,

I. I am the Lord thy God, which have brought thee out of the land of Egypt, out of the house of bondage. Thou shalt have no other gods before me.

II. Thou shalt not make unto thee any graven image, or any likeness of any thing that is in heaven above, or that is in the earth beneath, or that is in the water under the earth: thou shalt not bow down thyself to them, nor serve them: for I the Lord thy God am a jealous God, visiting the iniquity of the fathers upon the children, unto the third and fourth generation of them that hate me, and showing mercy unto thousands of them that love me, and keep my commandments.

III. Thou shalt not take the name of the Lord thy God in vain; for the Lord will not hold him guiltless that taketh his name in vain.

IV. Remember the sabbath day, to keep it holy. Six days shalt thou labor, and do all thy work: but the seventh day is the sabbath of the Lord thy God: in it thou shalt not do any work, thou, nor thy son, nor thy daughter, thy manservant, nor thy maidservant, nor thy cattle, nor thy stranger that is within thy gates: for in six days the Lord made heaven and earth, the sea, and all that in them is, and rested the seventh day: wherefore the Lord blessed the sabbath day, and hallowed it.

V. Honor thy father and thy mother: that thy days may be long upon the land which the Lord thy God giveth thee.

VI. Thou shalt not kill.

VII. Thou shalt not commit adultery.

VIII. Thou shalt not steal.

IX. Thou shalt not bear false witness against thy neighbor.

X. Thou shalt not covet thy neighbor's house, thou shalt not covet thy neighbor's wife, nor his manservant, nor his maidservant, nor his ox, nor his ass, nor any thing that is thy neighbor's.

HEAR ALSO THE WORDS OF OUR LORD JESUS CHRIST:

[MATTHEW XXII: 37—40.]

Jesus said unto him, Thou shalt love the Lord thy God with all thy heart, and with all thy soul, and with all thy mind. This is the first and great commandment.

And the second is like unto it, Thou shalt love thy neighbor as thyself.

On these two commandments hang all the Law and the Prophets.

The Beatitudes.

[MATTHEW V : 3—12.]

BLESSED are the poor in spirit: for theirs is the kingdom of heaven.

Blessed are they that mourn : for they shall be comforted.

Blessed are the meek : for they shall inherit the earth.

Blessed are they which do hunger and thirst after righteousness: for they shall be filled.

Blessed are the merciful : for they shall obtain mercy.

Blessed are the pure in heart : for they shall see God.

Blessed are the peacemakers : for they shall be called the children of God.

Blessed are they which are persecuted for righteousness' sake : for theirs is the kingdom of heaven.

Blessed are ye, when men shall revile you, and persecute you, and shall say all manner of evil against you falsely, for my sake.

Rejoice, and be exceeding glad : for great is your reward in heaven : for so persecuted they the prophets which were before you.

"Blessed are they that do His commandments, that they may have right to the tree of life, and may enter in through the gates into the City."

NOTE.

THE following selections from the Psalms, and from other poetical parts of the Bible, are arranged to be read by the Minister and the People responsively, according to their original structure and design.

The lines printed in the Roman letter are to be read by the Minister.

The lines set inward from the margin, and printed in Italics, are to be read by the People.

Any lines printed in small Capitals are to be read by the Minister and the People together.

The selections are combined in Lessons, which experience has shown to be of a convenient length for use by Congregations; and those referring to one general subject are for the most part associated with each other.

The Index, at the end, refers to the page on which any Psalm, or other selection, may be found.

Order of Arrangement.

PSALMS:

		PAGES
I.	The Preparation of Spirit, for Divine Worship	11— 19
II.	The Worship of God, for His Goodness and Majesty	20— 63
III.	The Worship of God, for the Kingship of His Son	64— 67
IV.	The Worship of God, as Defender of His People	68— 85
V.	The Worship of God, as Judge in the Earth	86—105
VI.	The Worship of God, for the Teaching of His Word	106—109
VII.	Supplication to God, for Deliverance and Favor	110—129

OTHER SELECTIONS:

VIII.	Praise to God, for His Greatness	130—141
IX.	God's Purposes concerning Christ and the Church	142—155
X.	The Briefness of Man's Life	156—158
XI.	The Excellency of Wisdom	159—165
XII.	The Glory of the Heavenly Life	166—171

The Psalter.

Lesson 1. (Page 11.)

Psalm I.

BLESSED is the man that walketh not in the counsel of the ungodly,
  Nor standeth in the way of sinners,
  Nor sitteth in the seat of the scornful.
But his delight is in the law of the LORD;
  And in his law doth he meditate day and night.
And he shall be like a tree planted by the rivers of water,
  That bringeth forth his fruit in his season;
His leaf also shall not wither;
  And whatsoever he doeth shall prosper.
The ungodly are not so:
  But are like the chaff which the wind driveth away.
Therefore the ungodly shall not stand in the judgment,
  Nor sinners in the congregation of the righteous.
For the LORD knoweth the way of the righteous:
  But the way of the ungodly shall perish.

Psalm XV.

LORD, who shall abide in thy tabernacle?
  Who shall dwell in thy holy hill?
He that walketh uprightly, and worketh righteousness,
  And speaketh the truth in his heart.
He that backbiteth not with his tongue.
  Nor doeth evil to his neighbor,
  Nor taketh up a reproach against his neighbor.

In whose eyes a vile person is contemned;
But he honoreth them that fear the LORD.
He that sweareth to his own hurt, and changeth not.
He that putteth not out his money to usury,
Nor taketh reward against the innocent.
He that doeth these things shall never be moved.

PSALM XXVI.

JUDGE me, O LORD;
For I have walked in mine integrity:
I have trusted also in the LORD; *therefore I shall not slide.*
Examine me, O LORD, and prove me;
Try my reins and my heart.
For thy loving-kindness is before mine eyes:
And I have walked in thy truth.
I have not sat with vain persons,
Neither will I go in with dissemblers.
I have hated the congregation of evil doers;
And will not sit with the wicked.
I will wash mine hands in innocency:
So will I compass thine altar, O LORD:
That I may publish with the voice of thanksgiving,
And tell of all thy wondrous works.
LORD, I have loved the habitation of thine house,
And the place where thine honor dwelleth.
Gather not my soul with sinners,
Nor my life with bloody men:
In whose hands is mischief,
And their right hand is full of bribes.
But as for me, I will walk in mine integrity:
Redeem me, and be merciful unto me.
My foot standeth in an even place:
In the congregations will I bless the LORD.

Lesson 2. (Page 13.)

Psalm XXX.

I WILL extol thee, O Lord; for thou hast lifted me up,
    And hast not made my foes to rejoice over me.
O Lord my God, I cried unto thee,
    And thou hast healed me.
O Lord, thou hast brought up my soul from the grave:
    Thou hast kept me alive, that I should not go down to the pit.
Sing unto the Lord, O ye saints of his,
    And give thanks at the remembrance of his holiness.
For his anger endureth but a moment; in his favor is life;
    Weeping may endure for a night, but joy cometh in the morning.
And in my prosperity I said, I shall never be moved.
    Lord, by thy favor thou hast made my mountain to stand strong.
Thou didst hide thy face, and I was troubled.
    I cried to thee, O Lord; and unto the Lord I made supplication.
What profit is there in my blood, when I go down to the pit?
    Shall the dust praise thee? shall it declare thy truth?
Hear, O Lord, and have mercy upon me:
    Lord, be thou my helper.
Thou hast turned for me my mourning into dancing:
    Thou hast put off my sackcloth, and girded me with gladness;
To the end that my glory may sing praise to thee, and not be silent.
    O Lord, my God, I will give thanks unto thee for ever.

Psalm XXVIII.

UNTO thee will I cry, O Lord my rock; be not silent to me:
    Lest, if thou be silent to me, I become like them that go down into the pit.
Hear the voice of my supplications, when I cry unto thee,
    When I lift up my hands toward thy holy oracle.
Draw me not away with the wicked, and with the workers of iniquity.
    Which speak peace to their neighbors, but mischief is in their hearts.
Give them according to their deeds,
    And according to the wickedness of their endeavors:
Give them after the work of their hands;
    Render to them their desert.

{ Because they regard not the works of the LORD,
{ Nor the operation of his hands,
> He shall destroy them, and not build them up.

Blessed be the LORD,
> Because he hath heard the voice of my supplications.

The LORD is my strength and my shield;
> My heart trusted in him, and I am helped:

Therefore my heart greatly rejoiceth;
> And with my song will I praise him.

The LORD is their strength,
> And he is the saving strength of his anointed.

Save thy people, and bless thine heritage:
> Feed them also, and lift them up for ever.

PSALM CXII.

PRAISE ye the LORD. Blessed is the man that feareth the LORD,
> That delighteth greatly in his commandments.

His seed shall be mighty upon earth:
> The generation of the upright shall be blessed.

Wealth and riches shall be in his house:
> And his righteousness endureth for ever.

Unto the upright there ariseth light in the darkness:
> He is gracious, and full of compassion, and righteous.

A good man showeth favor, and lendeth;
> He will guide his affairs with discretion.

Surely he shall not be moved for ever:
> The righteous shall be in everlasting remembrance.

He shall not be afraid of evil tidings:
> His heart is fixed, trusting in the LORD.

His heart is established, he shall not be afraid,
> Until he see his desire upon his enemies.

He hath dispersed, he hath given to the poor:
> His righteousness endureth for ever; his horn shall be exalted with honor.

The wicked shall see it, and be grieved;
> { He shall gnash with his teeth, and melt away:
> { The desire of the wicked shall perish.

Lesson 3. (Page 15.)

Psalm XXXIV.

I WILL bless the Lord at all times:
His praise shall continually be in my mouth.
My soul shall make her boast in the Lord:
The humble shall hear thereof, and be glad.
Oh magnify the Lord with me,
And let us exalt his name together.
I sought the Lord, and he heard me,
And delivered me from all my fears.
They looked unto him, and were lightened:
And their faces were not ashamed.
This poor man cried, and the Lord heard him,
And saved him out of all his troubles.
The angel of the Lord encampeth round about them that fear him,
And delivereth them.
O taste and see that the Lord is good:
Blessed is the man that trusteth in him.
Oh fear the Lord, ye his saints:
For there is no want to them that fear him.
The young lions do lack, and suffer hunger:
But they that seek the Lord shall not want any good thing.
Come, ye children, hearken unto me:
I will teach you the fear of the Lord.
What man is he that desireth life,
And loveth many days, that he may see good?
Keep thy tongue from evil,
And thy lips from speaking guile.
Depart from evil, and do good;
Seek peace, and pursue it.
The eyes of the Lord are upon the righteous,
And his ears are open unto their cry.
The face of the Lord is against them that do evil,
To cut off the remembrance of them from the earth.
The righteous cry, and the Lord heareth,
And delivereth them out of all their troubles.
The Lord is nigh unto them that are of a broken heart;
And saveth such as be of a contrite spirit.

Many are the afflictions of the righteous:
   But the Lord delivereth him out of them all.
He keepeth all his bones:
   Not one of them is broken.
Evil shall slay the wicked:
   And they that hate the righteous shall be desolate.
The Lord redeemeth the soul of his servants;
   And none of them that trust in him shall be desolate.

Psalm CXXVI.

WHEN the Lord turned again the captivity of Zion,
   We were like them that dream.
Then was our mouth filled with laughter,
   And our tongue with singing:
Then said they among the heathen,
   The Lord hath done great things for them.
The Lord hath done great things for us;
   Whereof we are glad.
Turn again our captivity, O Lord,
   As the streams in the south.
They that sow in tears
   Shall reap in joy.
He that goeth forth and weepeth, bearing precious seed,
   { *Shall doubtless come again with rejoicing,*
   { *Bringing his sheaves with him.*

Lesson 4. (Page 16.)

Psalm XLII.

AS the hart panteth after the water brooks,
   So panteth my soul after thee, O God.
My soul thirsteth for God, for the living God:
   When shall I come and appear before God?
My tears have been my meat day and night,
   While they continually say unto me, Where is thy God?
When I remember these things I pour out my soul in me:
   { *For I had gone with the multitude, I went with them to the house of God,*
   { *With the voice of joy and praise, with a multitude that kept holyday.*

Why art thou cast down, O my soul? and why art thou disquieted in me?
> Hope thou in God: for I shall yet praise him,
> For the help of his countenance.

O my God, my soul is cast down within me: therefore will I remember thee,
> From the land of Jordan, and of the Hermonites, from the hill Mizar.

Deep calleth unto deep at the noise of thy waterspouts:
> All thy waves and thy billows are gone over me.

Yet the LORD will command his loving-kindness in the daytime,
> And in the night his song shall be with me, and my prayer unto the God of my life.

I will say unto God, my rock, Why hast thou forgotten me?
> Why go I mourning because of the oppression of the enemy?

As with a sword in my bones, mine enemies reproach me;
> While they say daily unto me, Where is thy God?

Why art thou cast down, O my soul? and why art thou disquieted within me?
> Hope thou in God: for I shall yet praise him,
> Who is the health of my countenance, and my God.

Psalm XLIII.

JUDGE me, O God, and plead my cause against an ungodly nation:
> Oh deliver me from the deceitful and unjust man.

For thou art the God of my strength: why dost thou cast me off?
> Why go I mourning because of the oppression of the enemy?

Oh send out thy light and thy truth: let them lead me;
> Let them bring me unto thy holy hill, and to thy tabernacles;

Then will I go unto the altar of God, unto God my exceeding joy:
> Yea, upon the harp will I praise thee, O God, my God.

Why art thou cast down, O my soul? and why art thou disquieted within me?
> Hope in God: for I shall yet praise him,
> Who is the health of my countenance, and my God.

Psalm XLVI.

GOD is our refuge and strength,
> A very present help in trouble.

Therefore will not we fear, though the earth be removed,
> And though the mountains be carried into the midst of the sea;

Though the waters thereof roar and be troubled,
> Though the mountains shake with the swelling thereof.

There is a river, the streams whereof shall make glad the city of God;
> The holy place of the tabernacles of the Most High.

God is in the midst of her; she shall not be moved;
> God shall help her, and that right early.

The heathen raged, the kingdoms were moved:
    He uttered his voice, the earth melted.
The LORD of hosts is with us;
    The God of Jacob is our refuge.
Come, behold the works of the LORD,
    What desolations he hath made in the earth.
He maketh wars to cease, unto the ends of the earth;
    { *He breaketh the bow, and cutteth the spear in sunder;*
    { *He burneth the chariot in the fire.*
Be still, and know that I am God;
    I will be exalted among the heathen, I will be exalted in the earth.
The LORD of hosts is with us;
    The God of Jacob is our refuge.

Lesson 5. (PAGE 18.)

PSALM LI.

HAVE mercy upon me, O God, according to thy loving-kindness:
    According unto the multitude of thy tender mercies, blot out my transgressions.
Wash me thoroughly from mine iniquity,
    And cleanse me from my sin.
For I acknowledge my transgressions:
    And my sin is ever before me.
Against thee, thee only, have I sinned,
    And done this evil in thy sight:
That thou mightest be justified when thou speakest,
    And be clear when thou judgest.
Behold, I was shapen in iniquity,
    And in sin did my mother conceive me.
Behold thou desirest truth in the inward parts:
    And in the hidden part thou shalt make me to know wisdom.
Purge me with hyssop, and I shall be clean:
    Wash me, and I shall be whiter than snow.
Make me to hear joy and gladness;
    That the bones which thou hast broken may rejoice.
Hide thy face from my sins,
    And blot out all mine iniquities.

Create in me a clean heart, O God ;
And renew a right spirit within me.
Cast me not away from thy presence ;
And take not thy Holy Spirit from me.
Restore unto me the joy of thy salvation ;
And uphold me with thy free Spirit.
Then will I teach transgressors thy ways ;
And sinners shall be converted unto thee.
Deliver me from blood guiltiness, O God, thou God of my salvation :
And my tongue shall sing aloud of thy righteousness.
O LORD, open thou my lips ;
And my mouth shall show forth thy praise.
For thou desirest not sacrifice ; else would I give it :
Thou delightest not in burnt offering.
The sacrifices of God are a broken spirit :
A broken and a contrite heart, O God, thou wilt not despise.
Do good in thy good pleasure unto Zion :
Build thou the walls of Jerusalem.
Then shalt thou be pleased with the sacrifices of righteousness,
{ With burnt offering and whole burnt offering :
{ Then shall they offer bullocks upon thine altar.

PSALM CXXX.

OUT of the depths have I cried unto thee, O LORD. LORD, hear my voice:
Let thine ears be attentive to the voice of my supplications.
If thou, LORD, shouldest mark iniquity, O LORD, who shall stand ?
But there is forgiveness with thee, that thou mayest be feared.
I wait for the LORD, my soul doth wait,
And in his word do I hope.
My soul waiteth for the LORD, more than they that watch for the morning :
I say, more than they that watch for the morning.
Let Israel hope in the LORD :
For with the LORD there is mercy,
And with him is plenteous redemption,
And he shall redeem Israel from all his iniquities.

Lesson 6. (Page 20.)

Psalm CIII.

BLESS the LORD, O my soul;
  And all that is within me, bless his holy name.
Bless the LORD, O my soul;
  And forget not all his benefits;
Who forgiveth all thine iniquities:
  Who healeth all thy diseases;
Who redeemeth thy life from destruction:
  Who crowneth thee with loving-kindness and tender mercies;
Who satisfieth thy mouth with good things:
  So that thy youth is renewed like the eagle's.
The LORD executeth righteousness,
  And judgment for all that are oppressed.
He made known his ways unto Moses,
  His acts unto the children of Israel.
The LORD is merciful and gracious,
  Slow to anger and plenteous in mercy.
He will not always chide:
  Neither will he keep his anger for ever.
He hath not dealt with us after our sins;
  Nor rewarded us according to our iniquities.
For as the heaven is high above the earth,
  So great is his mercy toward them that fear him.
As far as the east is from the west,
  So far hath he removed our transgressions from us.
Like as a father pitieth his children,
  So the LORD pitieth them that fear him.
For he knoweth our frame;
  He remembereth that we are dust.
As for man, his days are as grass:
  As a flower of the field, so he flourisheth.
For the wind passeth over it, and it is gone;
  And the place thereof shall know it no more.
But the mercy of the LORD is from everlasting to everlasting upon them that fear him,
  And his righteousness unto children's children;

To such as keep his covenant,
 And to those that remember his commandments to do them.
The LORD hath prepared his throne in the heavens;
 And his kingdom ruleth over all.
Bless the LORD, ye his angels, that excel in strength,
 That do his commandments, hearkening unto the voice of his word.
Bless ye the LORD, all ye his hosts;
 Ye ministers of his, that do his pleasure.
Bless the LORD, all his works, in all places of his dominion:
 Bless the LORD, O my soul.

Psalm CXI.

PRAISE ye the LORD.
 { I will praise the LORD with my whole heart,
 { In the assembly of the upright, and in the congregation.
The works of the LORD are great,
 Sought out of all them that have pleasure therein.
His work is honorable and glorious:
 And his righteousness endureth for ever.
He hath made his wonderful works to be remembered:
 The LORD is gracious, and full of compassion.
He hath given meat unto them that fear him:
 He will ever be mindful of his covenant.
He hath shewed his people the power of his works;
 That he may give them the heritage of the heathen.
The works of his hands are verity and judgment;
 All his commandments are sure.
They stand fast for ever and ever;
 And are done in truth and uprightness.
He sent redemption unto his people:
 { He hath commanded his covenant for ever:
 { Holy and reverend is his name.
The fear of the LORD is the beginning of wisdom:
 { A good understanding have all they that do his commandments:
 { His praise endureth for ever.

Lesson 7. (Page 22.)

Psalm XIX.

THE heavens declare the glory of God;
 And the firmament sheweth his handywork.
Day unto day uttereth speech,
 And night unto night sheweth knowledge.
There is no speech nor language,
 Where their voice is not heard.
Their line is gone out through all the earth,
 And their words to the end of the world.
In them hath he set a tabernacle for the sun,
 { Which is as a bridegroom coming out of his chamber,
 { And rejoiceth as a strong man to run a race.
His going forth is from the end of the heaven,
 { And his circuit unto the ends of it :
 { And there is nothing hid from the heat thereof.
The law of the Lord is perfect, converting the soul:
 The testimony of the Lord is sure, making wise the simple.
The statutes of the Lord are right, rejoicing the heart :
 The commandment of the Lord is pure, enlightening the eyes.
The fear of the Lord is clean, enduring for ever :
 The judgments of the Lord are true and righteous altogether.
More to be desired are they than gold, yea, than much fine gold:
 Sweeter also than honey, and the honeycomb.
Moreover by them is thy servant warned:
 And in keeping of them there is great reward.
Who can understand his errors ?
 Cleanse thou me from secret faults.
Keep back thy servant also from presumptuous sins ; let them not have dominion over me :
 Then shall I be upright, and I shall be innocent from the great transgression.
Let the words of my mouth, and the meditation of my heart, be acceptable in thy sight,
 O Lord, my Strength, and my Redeemer.

Psalm VIII.

O LORD our LORD,
  How excellent is thy name in all the earth!
  Who hast set thy glory above the heavens.
Out of the mouth of babes and sucklings hast thou ordained strength,
  Because of thine enemies,
  That thou mightest still the enemy and the avenger.
When I consider thy heavens, the work of thy fingers,
  The moon and the stars, which thou hast ordained;
What is man, that thou art mindful of him?
  And the son of man, that thou visitest him?
For thou hast made him a little lower than the angels,
  And hast crowned him with glory and honor.
Thou madest him to have dominion over the work of thy hands;
  Thou hast put all things under his feet:
All sheep and oxen,
  Yea, and the beasts of the field;
The fowl of the air, and the fish of the sea,
  And whatsoever passeth through the paths of the seas.
O LORD, our LORD,
  How excellent is thy name in all the earth!

Psalm XVI.

PRESERVE me, O God:
  For in thee do I put my trust.
O my soul, thou hast said unto the LORD, Thou art my LORD:
  My goodness extendeth not to thee;
But to the saints that are in the earth,
  And to the excellent, in whom is all my delight.
Their sorrows shall be multiplied that hasten after another god:
  Their drink offerings of blood will I not offer,
  Nor take up their names into my lips.
The LORD is the portion of mine inheritance and of my cup:
  Thou maintainest my lot.
The lines are fallen unto me in pleasant places;
  Yea, I have a goodly heritage.
I will bless the LORD, who hath given me counsel:
  My reins also instruct me in the night seasons.
I have set the LORD always before me:
  Because he is at my right hand, I shall not be moved.

Therefore my heart is glad, and my glory rejoiceth ;
My flesh also shall rest in hope.
For thou wilt not leave my soul in hell ;
Neither wilt thou suffer thine Holy One to see corruption.
Thou wilt show me the path of life :
*{ In thy presence is fulness of joy ;
At thy right hand there are pleasures for evermore.*

Lesson 8. (Page 24.)

Psalm XXIII.

THE Lord is my shepherd ;
I shall not want.
He maketh me to lie down in green pastures :
He leadeth me beside the still waters.
He restoreth my soul :
He leadeth me in the paths of righteousness, for his name's sake.
{ Yea, though I walk through the valley of the shadow of death,
I will fear no evil :
For thou art with me ; thy rod and thy staff they comfort me.
Thou preparest a table before me in the presence of mine enemies :
Thou anointest my head with oil ; my cup runneth over.
Surely goodness and mercy shall follow me all the days of my life :
And I will dwell in the house of the Lord for ever.

Psalm XXIV.

THE earth is the Lord's and the fulness thereof ;
The world, and they that dwell therein.
For he hath founded it upon the seas,
And established it upon the floods.
Who shall ascend into the hill of the Lord ?
And who shall stand in his holy place ?
He that hath clean hands, and a pure heart ;
Who hath not lifted up his soul unto vanity, nor sworn deceitfully.
He shall receive the blessing from the Lord,
And righteousness from the God of his salvation.
This is the generation of them that seek him,
That seek thy face, O Jacob.

Lift up your heads, O ye gates ;
> And be ye lifted up, ye everlasting doors ;
> And the King of glory shall come in.

Who is this King of glory?
> *The* Lord *strong and mighty, the* Lord *mighty in battle.*

Lift up your heads, O ye gates ;
> *Even lift them up, ye everlasting doors ;*
> *And the King of glory shall come in.*

Who is this King of glory?
> *The* Lord *of hosts, He is the King of glory.*

Psalm XXVII.

THE Lord is my light and my salvation ; whom shall I fear ?
> *The* Lord *is the strength of my life ; of whom shall I be afraid?*

When the wicked, even mine enemies and my foes, came upon me to eat up my flesh,
> *They stumbled and fell.*

Though a host should encamp against me, my heart shall not fear ;
> *Though war should rise against me, in this will I be confident.*

One thing have I desired of the Lord, that will I seek after ;
> *That I may dwell in the house of the* Lord *all the days of my life,*
> *To behold the beauty of the* Lord, *and to inquire in his temple.*

For in the time of trouble he shall hide me in his pavilion :
> *In the secret of his tabernacle shall he hide me ;*
> *He shall set me up upon a rock.*

And now shall mine head be lifted up above mine enemies round about me :
> *Therefore will I offer in his tabernacle sacrifices of joy ;*
> *I will sing, yea, I will sing praises unto the* Lord.

Hear, O Lord, when I cry with my voice :
> *Have mercy also upon me, and answer me.*

When thou saidst, Seek ye my face ;
> *My heart said unto thee, Thy face,* Lord, *will I seek.*

Hide not thy face far from me ; put not thy servant away in anger:
> *Thou hast been my help ;*
> *Leave me not, neither forsake me, O God of my salvation.*

When my father and my mother forsake me,
> *Then the* Lord *will take me up.*

Teach me thy way, O Lord,
> *And lead me in a plain path, because of mine enemies.*

Deliver me not over unto the will of mine enemies :
> *For false witnesses are risen up against me, and such as breathe out cruelty.*

I had fainted unless I had believed to see the goodness of the LORD in the land of the living.

Wait on the LORD:

Be of good courage, and he shall strengthen thine heart :

Wait, I say, on the LORD.

Lesson 9. (PAGE 26.)

PSALM V.

GIVE ear to my words, O LORD ;
Consider my meditation.
Hearken unto the voice of my cry, my King and my God :
For unto thee will I pray.
My voice shalt thou hear in the morning, O LORD ;
In the morning will I direct my prayer unto thee, and will look up.
For thou art not a God that hath pleasure in wickedness:
Neither shall evil dwell with thee.
The foolish shall not stand in thy sight :
Thou hatest all workers of iniquity.
Thou shalt destroy them that speak leasing :
The LORD *will abhor the bloody and deceitful man.*
But as for me, I will come into thy house in the multitude of thy mercy :
And in thy fear will I worship toward thy holy temple.
Lead me, O LORD, in thy righteousness, because of mine enemies ;
Make thy way straight before my face.
For there is no faithfulness in their mouth ; their inward part is very wickedness.
Their throat is an open sepulchre ; they flatter with their tongue.
Destroy thou them, O God ; let them fall by their own counsels ;
Cast them out in the multitude of their transgressions; for they have rebelled against thee.
But let all those that put their trust in thee rejoice:
{ *Let them ever shout for joy, because thou defendest them :*
{ *Let them also that love thy name be joyful in thee.*
For thou, LORD, wilt bless the righteous ;
With favor wilt thou compass him as with a shield.

Psalm XXXIII.

REJOICE in the LORD, O ye righteous:
For praise is comely for the upright.
Praise the LORD with the harp:
Sing unto him with the psaltery, and an instrument of ten strings.
Sing unto him a new song;
Play skillfully with a loud noise.
For the word of the LORD is right;
And all his works are done in truth,
He loveth righteousness and judgment:
The earth is full of the goodness of the LORD.
By the word of the LORD were the heavens made;
And all the host of them by the breath of his mouth.
He gathereth the waters of the sea together as a heap:
He layeth up the depth in storehouses.
Let all the earth fear the LORD:
Let all the inhabitants of the world stand in awe of him.
For he spake and it was done:
He commanded, and it stood fast.
The LORD bringeth the counsel of the heathen to nought:
He maketh the devices of the people of none effect.
The counsel of the LORD standeth forever,
The thoughts of his heart to all generations.
Blessed is the nation whose God is the LORD;
And the people whom he hath chosen for his own inheritance.
The LORD looketh from heaven;
He beholdeth all the sons of men.
From the place of his habitation he looketh,
Upon all the inhabitants of the earth.
He fashioneth their hearts alike;
He considereth all their works.
There is no king saved by the multitude of a host:
A mighty man is not delivered by much strength.
A horse is a vain thing for safety:
Neither shall he deliver any by his great strength.
Behold, the eye of the LORD is upon them that fear him,
Upon them that hope in his mercy;
To deliver their soul from death,
And to keep them alive in famine.
Our soul waiteth for the LORD:
He is our help and our shield.

For our heart shall rejoice in him,
  Because we have trusted in his holy name.
Let thy mercy, O Lord, be upon us,
  According as we hope in thee.

Lesson 10. (Page 28.)

Psalm XLVIII.

GREAT is the Lord, and greatly to be praised,
  In the city of our God, in the mountain of his holiness.
Beautiful for situation, the joy of the whole earth, is Mount Zion,
  On the sides of the north, the city of the great King.
God is known in her palaces for a refuge.
  For, lo, the kings were assembled, they passed by together.
They saw it, and so they marvelled;
  They were troubled, and hasted away.
Fear took hold upon them there, and pain, as of a woman in travail.
  Thou breakest the ships of Tarshish with an east wind.
As we have heard, so have we seen, in the city of the Lord of hosts,
  In the city of our God: God will establish it for ever.
We have thought of thy loving-kindness, O God,
  In the midst of thy temple.
According to thy name, O God, so is thy praise, unto the ends of the earth:
  Thy right hand is full of righteousness.
Let Mount Zion rejoice,
  Let the daughters of Judah be glad, because of thy judgments.
Walk about Zion, and go round about her:
  Tell the towers thereof:
Mark ye well her bulwarks, consider her palaces;
  That ye may tell it to the generation following.
For this God is our God for ever and ever;
  He will be our guide, even unto death.

Psalm LXIII.

O GOD, thou art my God; early will I seek thee: my soul thirsteth for thee:
  My flesh longeth for thee in a dry and thirsty land, where no water is;
To see thy power and thy glory,
  So as I have seen thee in the sanctuary.

Because thy loving-kindness is better than life,
  My lips shall praise thee.
Thus will I bless thee while I live :
  I will lift up my hands in thy name.
My soul shall be satisfied as with marrow and fatness;
  And my mouth shall praise thee with joyful lips.
When I remember thee upon my bed,
  And meditate on thee in the night watches.
Because thou hast been my help,
  Therefore in the shadow of thy wings will I rejoice.
My soul followeth hard after thee :
  Thy right hand upholdeth me.
But those that seek my soul to destroy it,
  Shall go into the lower parts of the earth.
They shall fall by the sword:
  They shall be a portion for foxes.
But the king shall rejoice in God;
  { *Every one that sweareth by him shall glory :*
  { *But the mouth of them that speak lies shall be stopped.*

Psalm LXXXIV.

HOW amiable are thy tabernacles,
  O LORD of hosts!
My soul longeth, yea, even fainteth for the courts of the LORD:
  My heart and my flesh crieth out for the living God.
Yea, the sparrow hath found a house,
  And the swallow a nest for herself, where she may lay her young.
Even thine altars, O LORD of hosts,
  My King and my God.
Blessed are they that dwell in thy house:
  They will be still praising thee.
Blessed is the man whose strength is in thee;
  In whose heart are the ways of them.
Who passing through the valley of Baca make it a well:
  The rain also filleth the pools.
They go from strength to strength,
  Every one of them in Zion appeareth before God.
O LORD God of hosts, hear my prayer:
  Give ear, O God of Jacob.
Behold, O God our shield,
  And look upon the face of thine anointed.

For a day in thy courts is better than a thousand.
> I had rather be a doorkeeper in the house of my God,
> Than to dwell in the tents of wickedness.

For the LORD God is a sun and shield:
> The LORD will give grace and glory;
> No good thing will he withhold from them that walk uprightly.

O LORD of hosts,
Blessed is the man that trusteth in thee.

Lesson 11. (PAGE 30.)

PSALM LXV.

PRAISE waiteth for thee, O God, in Zion:
And unto thee shall the vow be performed.
O thou that hearest prayer, unto thee shall all flesh come.
> Iniquities prevail against me:
> As for our transgressions, thou shalt purge them away.

Blessed is the man whom thou choosest, and causest to approach unto thee,
that he may dwell in thy courts:
We shall be satisfied with the goodness of thy house, even of thy holy temple.
By terrible things in righteousness wilt thou answer us, O God of our salvation:
Who art the confidence of all the ends of the earth, and of them that are
afar off upon the sea.
Which by his strength setteth fast the mountains; being girded with power:
> Which stilleth the noise of the seas, the noise of their waves,
> And the tumult of the people.

They also that dwell in the uttermost parts are afraid at thy tokens:
Thou makest the outgoings of the morning and evening to rejoice.
Thou visitest the earth, and waterest it:·
Thou greatly enrichest it,
With the river of God, which is full of water:
Thou preparest them corn, when thou hast so provided for it.
Thou waterest the ridges thereof abundantly, thou settlest the furrows thereof:
Thou makest it soft with showers, thou blessest the springing thereof.
Thou crownest the year with thy goodness;
And thy paths drop fatness.
They drop upon the pastures of the wilderness:
And the little hills rejoice on every side.

The pastures are clothed with flocks;
  { *The valleys also are covered over with corn*
  { *They shout for joy, they also sing.*

Psalm LXVI.

MAKE a joyful noise unto God, all ye lands:
  Sing forth the honor of his name: make his praise glorious.
Say unto God, How terrible art thou in thy works!
  Through the greatness of thy power shall thine enemies submit themselves unto thee.
All the earth shall worship thee, and shall sing unto thee;
  They shall sing to thy name.
Come and see the works of God:
  He is terrible in his doing toward the children of men.
He turned the sea into dry land:
  They went through the flood on foot: there did we rejoice in him.
He ruleth by his power forever; his eyes behold the nations:
  Let not the rebellious exalt themselves.
Oh bless our God, ye people,
  And make the voice of his praise to be heard:
Which holdeth our soul in life,
  And suffereth not our feet to be moved.
For thou, O God, hast proved us:
  Thou hast tried us as silver is tried.
Thou broughtest us into the net;
  Thou laidst affliction upon our loins.
Thou hast caused men to ride over our heads;
  { *We went through fire and through water:*
  { *But thou broughtest us out into a wealthy place.*
I will go into thy house with burnt offerings:
  I will pay thee my vows,
Which my lips have uttered,
  And my mouth hath spoken, when I was in trouble.
I will offer unto thee burnt sacrifices of fatlings,
  With the incense of rams: I will offer bullocks with goats.
Come and hear, all ye that fear God,
  And I will declare what he hath done for my soul.
I cried unto him with my mouth,
  And he was extolled with my tongue.
If I regard iniquity in my heart,
  The Lord *will not hear me:*

But verily God hath heard me;
He hath attended to the voice of my prayer.
Blessed be God, which hath not turned away my prayer,
Nor his mercy from me.

Lesson 12. (PAGE 32.)

Psalm LXXXI.

SING aloud unto God our strength;
Make a joyful noise unto the God of Jacob.
Take a psalm, and bring hither the timbrel,
The pleasant harp with the psaltery.
Blow up the trumpet in the new moon,
In the time appointed, on our solemn feast day.
For this was a statute for Israel,
And a law of the God of Jacob.
This he ordained in Joseph for a testimony.
{ *When he went out through the land of Egypt:*
{ *Where I heard a language that I understood not.*
I removed his shoulder from the burden:
His hands were delivered from the pots.
Thou calledst in trouble, and I delivered thee;
{ *I answered thee in the secret place of thunder:*
{ *I proved thee at the waters of Meribah.*
Hear, O my people, and I will testify unto thee:
O Israel, if thou wilt hearken unto me;
There shall no strange God be in thee:
Neither shalt thou worship any strange God.
I am the LORD thy God, which brought thee out of the land of Egypt:
Open thy mouth wide, and I will fill it.
But my people would not hearken to my voice;
And Israel would none of me.
So I gave them up unto their own hearts' lust;
And they walked in their own counsels.
Oh that my people had hearkened unto me,
And Israel had walked in my ways!
I should soon have subdued their enemies,
And turned my hand against their adversaries.

The haters of the LORD should have submitted themselves unto him:
  But their time should have endured for ever.
He should have fed them also with the finest of the wheat :
  And with honey out of the rock should I have satisfied thee.

PSALM LXXXV.

LORD, thou hast been favorable unto thy land :
  Thou hast brought back the captivity of Jacob.
Thou hast forgiven the iniquity of thy people ;
  Thou hast covered all their sin.
Thou hast taken away all thy wrath:
  Thou hast turned thyself from the fierceness of thine anger.
Turn us, O God of our salvation,
  And cause thine anger toward us to cease.
Wilt thou be angry with us for ever ?
  Wilt thou draw out thine anger to all generations?
Wilt thou not revive us again :
  That thy people may rejoice in thee?
Shew us thy mercy, O LORD,
  And grant us thy salvation.
I will hear what God the LORD will speak :
  { For he will speak peace unto his people, and to his saints :
  { But let them not turn again to folly.
Surely his salvation is nigh them that fear him ;
  That glory may dwell in our land.
Mercy and truth are met together ;
  Righteousness and peace have kissed each other.
Truth shall spring out of the earth ;
  And righteousness shall look down from heaven.
Yea, the LORD shall give that which is good ;
  And our land shall yield her increase.
Righteousness shall go before him ;
  And shall set us in the way of his steps.

PSALM LXXXVII.

HIS foundation is in the holy mountains.
  { The LORD loveth the gates of Zion,
  { More than all the dwellings of Jacob.
Glorious things are spoken of thee,
  O city of God.
I will make mention of Rahab and Babylon to them that know me :
  Behold Philistia, and Tyre, with Ethiopia ; this man was born there.

And of Zion it shall be said, This and that man was born in her:
And the Highest himself shall establish her.
The LORD shall count, when he writeth up the people,
That this man was born there.
As well the singers as the players on instruments shall be there:
All my springs are in thee.

Lesson 13. (PAGE 34.)

PSALM LXXXVI.

BOW down thine ear, O LORD, and hear me:
For I am poor and needy.
Preserve my soul; for I am holy:
O thou my God, save thy servant that trusteth in thee.
Be merciful unto me, O LORD:
For I cry unto thee daily.
Rejoice the soul of thy servant:
For unto thee, O LORD, do I lift up my soul.
For thou, LORD, art good, and ready to forgive;
And plenteous in mercy, unto all them that call upon thee.
Give ear, O LORD, unto my prayer;
And attend to the voice of my supplications.
In the day of my trouble will I call upon thee:
For thou wilt answer me.
Among the gods there is none like unto thee, O LORD;
Neither are there any works like unto thy works.
All nations whom thou hast made shall come and worship before thee, O LORD;
And shall glorify thy name.
For thou art great, and doest wondrous things:
Thou art God alone.
Teach me thy way, O LORD; I will walk in thy truth:
Unite my heart to fear thy name.
I will praise thee, O LORD my God, with all my heart:
And I will glorify thy name for evermore.
For great is thy mercy toward me:
And thou hast delivered my soul from the lowest hell.

O God, the proud are risen against me,
: And the assemblies of violent men have sought after my soul;
: And have not set thee before them.
But thou, O LORD, art a God full of compassion, and gracious,
: Long-suffering, and plenteous in mercy and truth.
Oh turn unto me, and have mercy upon me;
: Give thy strength unto thy servant, and save the son of thine handmaid.
Shew me a token for good;
: That they which hate me may see it, and be ashamed:
: Because thou, LORD, hast holpen me, and comforted me.

Psalm XCII.

IT is a good thing to give thanks unto the LORD,
: And to sing praises unto thy name, O Most High:
To show forth thy loving-kindness in the morning,
: And thy faithfulness every night,
Upon an instrument of ten strings, and upon the psaltery;
: Upon the harp with a solemn sound.
For thou, LORD, hast made me glad through thy work:
: I will triumph in the works of thy hands.
O LORD, how great are thy works!
: And thy thoughts are very deep.
A brutish man knoweth not;
: Neither doth a fool understand this.
When the wicked spring as the grass,
: And when all the workers of iniquity do flourish;
It is that they shall be destroyed for ever:
: But thou, LORD, art most high for evermore.
For, lo, thine enemies, O LORD,
: For, lo, thine enemies shall perish;
: All the workers of iniquity shall be scattered.
But my horn shalt thou exalt like the horn of an unicorn:
: I shall be anointed with fresh oil.
Mine eye also shall see my desire on mine enemies,
: And mine ears shall hear my desire of the wicked that rise up against me
The righteous shall flourish like the palm tree;
: He shall grow like a cedar in Lebanon.
Those that be planted in the house of the LORD,
: Shall flourish in the courts of our God.
They shall still bring forth fruit in old age;
: They shall be fat and flourishing;
To show that the LORD is upright:
: He is my rock, and there is no unrighteousness in him.

Lesson 14. (Page 36.)

Psalm XCIII.

THE Lord reigneth,
  He is clothed with majesty;
The Lord is clothed with strength, wherewith he hath girded himself.
  The world also is stablished, that it cannot be moved.
Thy throne is established of old :
  Thou art from everlasting.
The floods have lifted up, O Lord,
  { *The floods have lifted up their voice.*
  { *The floods lift up their waves.*
The Lord on high is mightier than the noise of many waters,
  Yea, than the mighty waves of the sea.
Thy testimonies are very sure :
  Holiness becometh thine house, O Lord, *for ever.*

Psalm XCV.

OH come, let us sing unto the Lord :
  Let us make a joyful noise to the Rock of our Salvation.
Let us come before his presence with thanksgiving,
  And make a joyful noise unto him with psalms.
For the Lord is a great God,
  And a great King above all gods.
In his hand are the deep places of the earth :
  The strength of the hills is his also.
The sea is his, and he made it :
  And his hands formed the dry land.
Oh come, let us worship and bow down :
  Let us kneel before the Lord, *our maker.*
For he is our God ;
  And we are the people of his pasture, and the sheep of his hand.
To-day if ye will hear his voice, harden not your heart,
  { *As in the provocation,*
  { *And as in the day of temptation in the wilderness :*
When your fathers tempted me,
  Proved me, and saw my work.

Forty years long was I grieved with this generation,
  *And said, It is a people that do err in their heart,
  And they have not known my ways:*
Unto whom I sware in my wrath,
  That they should not enter into my rest.

Psalm XCVI.

OH sing unto the LORD a new song:
  Sing unto the LORD, all the earth,
Sing unto the LORD, bless his name;
  Show forth his salvation from day to day.
Declare his glory among the heathen,
  His wonders among all people.
For the LORD is great, and greatly to be praised:
  He is to be feared above all gods.
For all the gods of the nations are idols,
  But the LORD made the heavens.
Honor and majesty are before him:
  Strength and beauty are in his sanctuary.
Give unto the LORD, O ye kindreds of the people,
  Give unto the LORD glory and strength.
Give unto the LORD the glory due unto his name:
  Bring an offering, and come into his courts.
Oh worship the LORD in the beauty of holiness:
  Fear before him, all the earth.
Say among the heathen that the LORD reigneth:
  *The world also shall be established, that it shall not be moved:
  He shall judge the people righteously.*
Let the heavens rejoice, and the earth be glad;
  Let the sea roar, and the fulness thereof.
Let the field be joyful, and all that is therein:
  Then shall all the trees of the wood rejoice,
Before the LORD: for he cometh, for he cometh to judge the earth:
  *He shall judge the world with righteousness,
  And the people with his truth.*

Lesson 15. (Page 38.)

Psalm XCVII.

THE Lord reigneth: let the earth rejoice:
 Let the multitude of isles be glad thereof.
Clouds and darkness are round about him:
 Righteousness and judgment are the habitation of his throne.
A fire goeth before him,
 And burneth up his enemies round about.
His lightnings enlightened the world:
 The earth saw, and trembled.
The hills melted like wax at the presence of the Lord,
 At the presence of the Lord of the whole earth.
The heavens declare his righteousness,
 And all the people see his glory.
Confounded be all they that serve graven images,
 That boast themselves of idols: worship him, all ye gods.
Zion heard, and was glad;
 { *And the daughters of Judah rejoiced,*
 { *Because of thy judgments, O Lord.*
For thou, Lord, art high above all the earth:
 Thou art exalted far above all gods.
Ye that love the Lord, hate evil:
 { *He preserveth the souls of his saints;*
 { *He delivereth them out of the hand of the wicked.*
Light is sown for the righteous,
 And gladness for the upright in heart.
Rejoice in the Lord, ye righteous;
 And give thanks at the remembrance of his holiness.

Psalm XCVIII.

OH sing unto the Lord a new song; for he hath done marvellous things
 His right hand, and his holy arm, hath gotten him the victory.
The Lord hath made known his salvation:
 His righteousness hath he openly showed in the sight of the heathen.
He hath remembered his mercy and his truth toward the house of Israel:
 All the ends of the earth have seen the salvation of our God.
Make a joyful noise unto the Lord, all the earth:
 Make a loud noise, and rejoice, and sing praise.
Sing unto the Lord with the harp;
 With the harp, and the voice of a psalm.

With trumpets, and sound of cornet,
  Make a joyful noise before the LORD, *the King.*
Let the sea roar, and the fulness thereof;
  The world, and they that dwell therein.
Let the floods clap their hands:
  Let the hills be joyful together,
Before the LORD; for he cometh to judge the earth;
  With righteousness shall he judge the world, and the people with equity.

PSALM XCIX.

THE LORD reigneth; let the people tremble:
  He sitteth between the cherubim; let the earth be moved.
The LORD is great in Zion;
  And he is high above all the people.
Let them praise thy great and terrible name;
  For it is holy.
The king's strength also loveth judgment;
  { *Thou dost establish equity,*
  { *Thou executest judgment and righteousness in Jacob.*
Exalt ye the LORD our God,
  And worship at his footstool; for he is holy.
Moses and Aaron among his priests,
  { *And Samuel among them that call upon his name;*
  { *They called upon the* LORD, *and he answered them.*
He spake unto them in the cloudy pillar:
  They kept his testimonies, and the ordinance that he gave them.
Thou answeredst them, O LORD our God:
  { *Thou wast a God that forgavest them,*
  { *Though thou tookest vengeance of their inventions.*
Exalt the LORD our God, and worship at his holy hill:
  For the LORD *our God is holy.*

PSALM C.

MAKE a joyful noise unto the LORD, all ye lands.
  Serve the LORD *with gladness: come before his presence with singing.*
Know ye that the LORD he is God:
  { *It is he that hath made us, and not we ourselves;*
  { *We are his people, and the sheep of his pasture.*
Enter into his gates with thanksgiving, and into his courts with praise:
  Be thankful unto him, and bless his name.
For the LORD is good; his mercy is everlasting;
  And his truth endureth to all generations.

Lesson 16. (Page 40.)

Psalm CIV.

BLESS the LORD, O my soul.
 { O LORD my God, thou art very great ;
 { Thou art clothed with honor and majesty.
Who coverest thyself with light as with a garment:
 Who stretchest out the heavens like a curtain:
Who layeth the beams of his chambers in the waters :
 { Who maketh the clouds his chariot :
 { Who walketh upon the wings of the wind :
Who maketh his angels spirits ;
 His ministers a flaming fire:
Who laid the foundations of the earth,
 That it should not be removed for ever.
Thou coveredst it with the deep as with a garment :
 The waters stood above the mountains.
At thy rebuke they fled ;
 At the voice of thy thunder they hasted away.
They go up by the mountains ;
 { *They go down by the valleys.*
 { *Unto the place which thou hast founded for them.*
Thou hast set a bound that they may not pass over ;
 That they turn not again to cover the earth.
He sendeth the springs into the valleys,
 Which run among the hills.
They give drink to every beast of the field :
 The wild asses quench their thirst.
By them shall the fowls of the heaven have their habitation,
 Which sing among the branches.
He watereth the hills from his chambers :
 The earth is satisfied with the fruit of thy works.
He causeth the grass to grow for the cattle,
 And herb for the service of man :
That he may bring forth food out of the earth ;
 And wine that maketh glad the heart of man,
And oil to make his face to shine,
 And bread which strengtheneth man's heart.
The trees of the LORD are full of sap ;
 The cedars of Lebanon, which he hath planted:

Where the birds make their nests :
As for the stork, the fir trees are her house,
The high hills are a refuge for the wild goats;
And the rocks for the conies.
He appointed the moon for seasons :
The sun knoweth his going down.
Thou makest darkness, and it is night :
Wherein all the beasts of the forest do creep forth.
The young lions roar after their prey,
And seek their meat from God.
The sun ariseth, they gather themselves together,
And lay them down in their dens.
Man goeth forth unto his work
And to his labor until the evening.
O LORD, how manifold are thy works!
In wisdom hast thou made them all : the earth is full of thy riches.
So is this great and wide sea, wherein are things creeping innumerable,
Both small and great beasts.
There go the ships :
There is that leviathan, whom thou hast made to play therein.
These wait all upon thee ;
That thou mayest give them their meat in due season.
That thou givest them they gather :
Thou openest thine hand, they are filled with good.
Thou hidest thy face, they are troubled :
Thou takest away their breath, they die, and return to their dust
Thou sendest forth thy spirit, they are created :
And thou renewest the face of the earth.
The glory of the LORD shall endure for ever :
The LORD shall rejoice in his works.
He looketh on the earth, and it trembleth :
He toucheth the hills, and they smoke.
I will sing unto the LORD as long as I live :
I will sing praises to my God while I have my being.
My meditation of him shall be sweet :
I will be glad in the LORD.
Let the sinners be consumed out of the earth,
And let the wicked be no more.
Bless thou the LORD, O my soul.
Praise ye the LORD.

Lesson 17. (Page 42.)

Psalm CV.

OH give thanks unto the LORD;
Call upon his name; make known his deeds among the people.
Sing unto him, sing psalms unto him:
Talk ye of all his wondrous works.
Glory ye in his holy name:
Let the heart of them rejoice that seek the LORD.
Seek the LORD, and his strength:
Seek his face evermore.
Remember his marvellous works that he hath done;
His wonders, and the judgments of his mouth;
O ye seed of Abraham his servant,
Ye children of Jacob his chosen.
He is the LORD our God:
His judgments are in all the earth.
He hath remembered his covenant for ever,
The word which he commanded, to a thousand generations.
Which covenant he made with Abraham,
And his oath unto Isaac:
And confirmed the same unto Jacob for a law,
And to Israel, for an everlasting covenant:
Saying, Unto thee will I give the land of Canaan,
The lot of your inheritance:
When they were but a few men in number;
Yea, very few, and strangers in it.
When they went from one nation to another,
From one kingdom to another people;
He suffered no man to do them wrong:
Yea, he reproved kings for their sakes;
Saying, Touch not mine anointed,
And do my prophets no harm.
Moreover he called for a famine upon the land:
He brake the whole staff of bread.
He sent a man before them,
Even Joseph, who was sold for a servant:
Whose feet they hurt with fetters:
He was laid in iron:

Until the time that his word came:
   The word of the LORD tried him.
The king sent and loosed him:
   Even the ruler of the people, and let him go free.
He made him lord of his house, and ruler of all his substance:
   To bind his princes at his pleasure, and teach his senators wisdom.
Israel also came into Egypt;
   And Jacob sojourned in the land of Ham.
And he increased his people greatly;
   And made them stronger than their enemies.
He turned their heart to hate his people,
   To deal subtilely with his servants.
He sent Moses, his servant;
   And Aaron whom he had chosen.
They showed his signs among them,
   And wonders in the land of Ham.
He sent darkness, and made it dark;
   And they rebelled not against his word.
He turned their waters into blood, and slew their fish.
   Their land brought forth frogs in abundance, in the chambers of their kings.
He spake, and there came divers sorts of flies, and lice in all their coasts.
   He gave them hail for rain, and flaming fire in their land.
He smote their vines also, and their fig trees; and brake the trees of their coasts.
   He spake, and the locusts came, and caterpillars, and that without number,
And did eat up all the herbs in their land,
   And devoured the fruit of their ground.
He smote also all the firstborn in their land,
   The chief of all their strength.
He brought them forth also with silver and gold;
   And there was not one feeble person among their tribes.
Egypt was glad when they departed:
   For the fear of them fell upon them.
He spread a cloud for a covering;
   And fire to give light in the night.
The people asked, and he brought quails,
   And satisfied them with the bread of heaven.
He opened the rock, and the waters gushed out;
   They ran in the dry places like a river.
For he remembered his holy promise,
   And Abraham, his servant.
And he brought forth his people with joy,
   And his chosen with gladness:

And gave them the lands of the heathen :
> *And they inherited the labor of the people ;*

That they might observe his statutes,
> *And keep his laws.* Praise ye the LORD.

Lesson 18. (PAGE 44.)

FROM PSALM CVI.

PRAISE ye the LORD.
> *O give thanks unto the LORD ; for he is good :*
> *For his mercy endureth for ever.*

Who can utter the mighty acts of the LORD ?
> *Who can show forth all his praise?*

Blessed are they that keep judgment,
> *And he that doeth righteousness at all times.*

Remember me, O LORD, with the favor that thou bearest unto thy people
> *O visit me with thy salvation ;*

That I may see the good of thy chosen,
> *That I may rejoice in the gladness of thy nation,*
> *That I may glory with thine inheritance.*

We have sinned with our fathers,
> *We have committed iniquity, we have done wickedly.*

Our fathers understood not thy wonders in Egypt ;
> *They remembered not the multitude of thy mercies ;*
> *But provoked him at the sea, even at the Red Sea.*

Nevertheless he saved them for his name's sake,
> *That he might make his mighty power to be known.*

He rebuked the Red Sea also, and it was dried up :
> *So he led them through the depths, as through the wilderness.*

And he saved them from the hand of him that hated them,
> *And redeemed them from the hand of the enemy.*

And the waters covered their enemies : there was not one of them left.
> *Then believed they his words ; they sang his praise.*

They soon forgat his works ; they waited not for his counsel :
> *But lusted exceedingly in the wilderness,*
> *And tempted God in the desert.*

And he gave them their request;
   But sent leanness into their soul.
They envied Moses also in the camp,
   And Aaron the saint of the LORD.
The earth opened, and swallowed up Dathan,
   And covered the company of Abiram.
And a fire was kindled in their company;
   The flame burned up the wicked.
They made a calf in Horeb,
   And worshipped the molten image.
Thus they changed their glory
   Into the similitude of an ox that eateth grass.
{ They forgat God their saviour,
{ Which had done great things in Egypt;
   { *Wondrous works in the land of Ham,*
   { *And terrible things by the Red Sea.*
Therefore he said that he would destroy them,
   { *Had not Moses his chosen stood before him in the breach,*
   { *To turn away his wrath, lest he should destroy them.*
Yea, they despised the pleasant land,
   They believed not his word;
But murmured in their tents,
   And hearkened not unto the voice of the LORD.
Therefore he lifted up his hand against them,
   To overthrow them in the wilderness;
To overthrow their seed also among the nations,
   And to scatter them in the lands.
They angered him also at the waters of strife,
   So that it went ill with Moses for their sakes:
Because they provoked his spirit,
   So that he spake unadvisedly with his lips.
{ They did not destroy the nations,
{ Concerning whom the LORD commanded them:
   { *But were mingled among the heathen,*
   { *And learned their works.*
{ And they served their idols:
{ Which were a snare unto them.
   { *Yea, they sacrificed their sons*
   { *And their daughters unto devils.*
{ And shed innocent blood,
{ Even the blood of their sons and of their daughters,
   { *Whom they sacrificed unto the idols of Canaan;*
   { *And the land was polluted with blood.*

Therefore was the wrath of the LORD kindled against his people,
> Insomuch that he abhorred his own inheritance.

And he gave them into the hand of the heathen;
> And they that hated them ruled over them.

Their enemies also oppressed them,
> And they were brought into subjection under their hand.

Many times did he deliver them;
> But they provoked him with their counsel,
> And were brought low for their iniquity.

Nevertheless he regarded their affliction,
> When he heard their cry:

And he remembered for them his covenant,
> And repented according to the multitude of his mercies.

He made them also to be pitied
> Of all those that carried them captives

Save us, O LORD our God, and gather us from among the heathen.
> To give thanks unto thy holy name, and to triumph in thy praise.

Blessed be the LORD God of Israel from everlasting to everlasting:
> And let all the people say, Amen. Praise ye the LORD.

Lesson 19. (PAGE 46.)

PSALM CVII.

OH give thanks unto the LORD, for he is good,
> For his mercy endureth for ever.

Let the redeemed of the LORD say so,
> Whom he hath redeemed from the hand of the enemy;

And gathered them out of the lands,
> From the east, and from the west, from the north, and from the south.

They wandered in the wilderness, in a solitary way;
> They found no city to dwell in.

Hungry and thirsty,
> Their soul fainted in them.

Then they cried unto the LORD in their trouble,
> And he delivered them out of their distresses.

And he led them forth by the right way,
> That they might go to a city of habitation.

Oh that men would praise the LORD for his goodness,
And for his wonderful works to the children of men;
For he satisfieth the longing soul,
And filleth the hungry soul with goodness.
Such as sit in darkness and the shadow of death,
Being bound in affliction and iron;
Because they rebelled against the words of God,
And contemned the counsel of the Most High:
Therefore he brought down their heart with labor;
They fell down: and there was none to help.
Then they cried unto the LORD in their trouble,
And he saved them out of their distresses.
He brought them out of darkness, and the shadow of death,
And brake their bands in sunder.
Oh that men would praise the LORD for his goodness,
And for his wonderful works to the children of men!
For he hath broken the gates of brass,
And cut the bars of iron in sunder.
Fools, because of their transgression,
And because of their iniquities, are afflicted.
Their soul abhorreth all manner of meat;
And they draw near unto the gates of death.
Then they cry unto the LORD in their trouble,
And he saveth them out of their distresses.
He sent his word, and healed them,
And delivered them from their destructions.
Oh that men would praise the LORD for his goodness.
And for his wonderful works to the children of men!
And let them sacrifice the sacrifices of thanksgiving,
And declare his works with rejoicing.
They that go down to the sea in ships,
That do business in great waters;
These see the works of the LORD,
And his wonders in the deep.
For he commandeth, and raiseth the stormy wind,
Which lifteth up the waves thereof.
They mount up to the heaven, they go down again to the depths;
Their soul is melted because of trouble.
They reel to and fro, and stagger like a drunken man.
And are at their wit's end.
Then they cry unto the Lord in their trouble,
And he bringeth them out of their distresses.

He maketh the storm a calm,
    So that the waves thereof are still.
Then are they glad, because they be quiet;
    So he bringeth them unto their desired haven.
Oh that men would praise the LORD for his goodness,
    And for his wonderful works to the children of men!
Let them exalt him also in the congregation of the people,
    And praise him in the assembly of the elders.
He turneth rivers into a wilderness,
    And the water-springs into dry ground;
A fruitful land into barrenness,
    For the wickedness of them that dwell therein.
He turneth the wilderness into a standing water,
    And the dry ground into water-springs:
And there he maketh the hungry to dwell,
    That they may prepare a city for habitation;
And sow the fields, and plant vineyards,
    Which may yield fruits of increase.
He blesseth them also, so that they are multiplied greatly;
    And suffereth not their cattle to decrease.
Again, they are minished and brought low,
    Through oppression, affliction, and sorrow.
He poureth contempt upon princes,
    And causeth them to wander in the wilderness, where there is no way.
Yet setteth he the poor on high from affliction,
    And maketh him families like a flock.
The righteous shall see it, and rejoice:
    And all iniquity shall stop her mouth.
Whoso is wise, and will observe these things,
    Even they shall understand the loving-kindness of the LORD.

Lesson 20. (PAGE 48.)

PSALM CVIII.

O GOD, my heart is fixed;
    I will sing and give praise, even with my glory.
Awake, psaltery and harp:
    I myself will awake early.

I will praise thee, O LORD, among the people:
  And I will sing praises unto thee among the nations.
For thy mercy is great above the heavens:
  And thy truth reacheth unto the clouds.
Be thou exalted, O God, above the heavens:
  And thy glory above all the earth;
That thy beloved may be delivered:
  Save with thy right hand, and answer me.
God hath spoken in his holiness; I will rejoice,
  I will divide Shechem, and mete out the valley of Succoth.
Gilead is mine; Manasseh is mine;
  Ephraim also is the strength of mine head; Judah is my lawgiver;
Moab is my washpot;
  Over Edom will I cast out my shoe; over Philistia will I triumph.
Who will bring me into the strong city?
  Who will lead me into Edom?
Wilt not thou, O God, who hast cast us off?
  And wilt not thou, O God, go forth with our hosts?
Give us help from trouble:
  For vain is the help of man.
Through God we shall do valiantly:
  For he it is that shall tread down our enemies.

PSALM CXVI.

I LOVE the LORD,
  Because he hath heard my voice and my supplications.
Because he hath inclined his ear unto me,
  Therefore will I call upon him as long as I live.
The sorrows of death compassed me,
  And the pains of hell gat hold upon me: I found trouble and sorrow
Then called I upon the name of the LORD;
  O LORD, I beseech thee, deliver my soul.
Gracious is the LORD, and righteous;
  Yea, our God is merciful.
The LORD preserveth the simple:
  I was brought low, and he helped me.
Return unto thy rest, O my soul;
  For the LORD hath dealt bountifully with thee.
For thou hast delivered my soul from death,
  Mine eyes from tears, and my feet from falling.
I will walk before the LORD in the land of the living.
  I believed, therefore have I spoken.

4

I was greatly afflicted:
I said in my haste, all men are liars.
What shall I render unto the LORD
For all his benefits toward me?
I will take the cup of salvation,
And call upon the name of the LORD.
I will pay my vows unto the LORD,
Now, in the presence of all his people.
Precious in the sight of the LORD is the death of his saints.
O LORD, truly I am thy servant;
I am thy servant, and the son of thine handmaid:
Thou hast loosed my bonds.
I will offer to thee the sacrifice of thanksgiving,
And will call upon the name of the LORD.
I will pay my vows unto the LORD,
Now, in the presence of all his people,
In the courts of the LORD'S house,
In the midst of thee, O Jerusalem.   Praise ye the LORD.

Lesson 21. (PAGE 50.)

PSALM CXIV.

WHEN Israel went out of Egypt,
The house of Jacob from a people of strange language;
Judah was his sanctuary,
And Israel his dominion.
The sea saw it, and fled:
Jordan was driven back.
The mountains skipped like rams,
And the little hills, like lambs.
What ailed thee, O thou sea, that thou fleddest?
Thou, Jordan, that thou wast driven back?
Ye mountains, that ye skipped like rams;
And ye little hills, like lambs?
Tremble, thou earth, at the presence of the LORD,
At the presence of the God of Jacob;
Which turned the rock into a standing water,
The flint into a fountain of waters.

Psalm CXIII.

PRAISE ye the LORD. Praise, O ye servants of the LORD,
Praise the name of the LORD.
Blessed be the name of the LORD,
From this time forth, and for evermore.
From the rising of the sun, unto the going down of the same,
The LORD'S *name is to be praised.*
The LORD is high above all nations,
And his glory above the heavens.
Who is like unto the LORD our God, who dwelleth on high;
Who humbleth himself to behold the things that are in heaven, and in the earth!
He raiseth up the poor out of the dust,
And lifteth the needy out of the dunghill;
That he may set him with princes,
Even with the princes of his people.
He maketh the barren woman to keep house,
And to be a joyful mother of children.
PRAISE YE THE LORD.

Psalm XXIX.

GIVE unto the LORD, O ye mighty,
Give unto the LORD *glory and strength.*
Give unto the LORD the glory due unto his name;
Worship the LORD *in the beauty of holiness.*
The voice of the LORD is upon the waters:
The God of glory thundereth: the LORD *is upon many waters.*
The voice of the LORD is powerful;
The voice of the LORD *is full of majesty.*
The voice of the LORD breaketh the cedars;
Yea, the LORD *breaketh the cedars of Lebanon.*
He maketh them also to skip like a calf;
Lebanon and Sirion like a young unicorn.
The voice of the LORD divideth the flames of fire.
{ *The voice of the* LORD *shaketh the wilderness;*
{ *The* LORD *shaketh the wilderness of Kadesh.*
{ The voice of the LORD maketh the hinds to calve;
{ And discovereth the forests:
And in his temple doth every one speak of his glory.
The LORD sitteth upon the flood;
Yea, the LORD *sitteth King forever.*
The LORD will give strength unto his people;
The LORD *will bless his people with peace.*

Lesson 22. (Page 52.)

Psalm CXVIII.

OH give thanks unto the Lord; for he is good:
   Because his mercy endureth for ever.
Let Israel now say,
   That his mercy endureth for ever.
Let the house of Aaron now say,
   That his mercy endureth for ever.
Let them now that fear the Lord say,
   That his mercy endureth for ever.
I called upon the Lord in distress:
   The Lord answered me, and set me in a large place.
The Lord is on my side; I will not fear:
   What can man do unto me?
The Lord taketh my part with them that help me:
   Therefore shall I see my desire upon them that hate me.
It is better to trust in the Lord than to put confidence in man.
   It is better to trust in the Lord than to put confidence in princes.
All nations compassed me about:
   But in the name of the Lord will I destroy them.
They compassed me about; yea, they compassed me about:
   But in the name of the Lord I will destroy them.
They compassed me about like bees;
   { *They are quenched as the fire of thorns:*
   { *For in the name of the Lord I will destroy them.*
Thou hast thrust sore at me that I might fall:
   But the Lord helped me.
The Lord is my strength and song,
   And is become my salvation.
The voice of rejoicing and salvation is in the tabernacles of the righteous:
   The right hand of the Lord doeth valiantly.
The right hand of the Lord is exalted:
   The right hand of the Lord doeth valiantly.
I shall not die, but live,
   And declare the works of the Lord.
The Lord hath chastened me sore:
   But he hath not given me over unto death.

Open to me the gates of righteousness :
I will go into them, and I will praise the LORD :
This gate of the LORD,
Into which the righteous shall enter.
I will praise thee : for thou hast heard me,
And art become my salvation.
The stone which the builders refused
Is become the head stone of the corner.
This is the LORD's doing ;
It is marvellous in our eyes.
This is the day which the LORD hath made ;
We will rejoice and be glad in it.
Save now, I beseech thee, O LORD :
O LORD, *I beseech thee, send now prosperity.*
Blessed be he that cometh in the name of the LORD :
We have blessed you out of the house of the LORD.
God is the LORD, which hath showed us light :
Bind the sacrifice with cords, even unto the horns of the altar.
Thou art my God, and I will praise thee :
Thou art my God, I will exalt thee.
Oh give thanks unto the LORD ; for he is good :
For his mercy endureth for ever.

PSALM CXVII.

O PRAISE the LORD, all ye nations :
Praise him, all ye people.
For his merciful kindness is great toward us :
And the truth of the LORD *endureth for ever. Praise ye the* LORD.

Lesson 23. (PAGE 53.)

PSALM CXXI.

I WILL lift up mine eyes unto the hills,
From whence cometh my help.
My help cometh from the LORD,
Which made heaven and earth.
He will not suffer thy foot to be moved :
He that keepeth thee will not slumber.

Behold, he that keepeth Israel
   Shall neither slumber nor sleep.
The LORD is thy keeper:
   The LORD is thy shade upon thy right hand.
The sun shall not smite thee by day,
   Nor the moon by night.
The LORD shall preserve thee from all evil
   He shall preserve thy soul.
The LORD shall preserve thy going out and thy coming in,
   From this time forth, and even for evermore.

PSALM CXXII.

I WAS glad when they said unto me,
   Let us go into the house of the LORD.
Our feet shall stand within thy gates, O Jerusalem.
   Jerusalem is builded as a city that is compact together:
Whither the tribes go up, the tribes of the LORD,
   Unto the testimony of Israel, to give thanks unto the name of the LORD.
For there are set thrones of judgment,
   The thrones of the house of David.
Pray for the peace of Jerusalem:
   They shall prosper that love thee.
Peace be within thy walls,
   And prosperity within thy palaces.
For my brethren and companions' sakes,
   I will now say, Peace be within thee.
Because of the house of the LORD our God,
   I will seek thy good.

PSALM CXXV.

THEY that trust in the LORD shall be as Mount Zion,
   Which cannot be removed, but abideth for ever.
As the mountains are round about Jerusalem,
   So the LORD is round about his people, from henceforth even for ever.
For the rod of the wicked shall not rest upon the lot of the righteous;
   Lest the righteous put forth their hands unto iniquity.
Do good, O LORD, unto those that be good,
   And to them that are upright in their hearts.
As for such as turn aside unto their crooked ways,
   { *The LORD shall lead them forth with the workers of iniquity.*
   { *But peace shall be upon Israel.*

Psalm CXXXIII.

BEHOLD, how good and how pleasant it is
For brethren to dwell together in unity.
It is like the precious ointment upon the head,
{ *That ran down upon the beard, even Aaron's beard:*
{ *That went down to the skirts of his garments!*
As the dew of Hermon, and as the dew that descended upon the mountains of Zion :
For there the LORD *commanded the blessing, even life for evermore.*

Psalm CXXXIV.

BEHOLD, bless ye the LORD, all ye servants of the LORD,
Which by night stand in the house of the LORD.
Lift up your hands in the sanctuary, and bless the LORD.
The LORD, *that made heaven and earth, bless thee out of Zion!*

Lesson 24. (PAGE 55.)

Psalm CXXXII.

LORD, remember David,
And all his afflictions;
How he sware unto the LORD,
And vowed unto the mighty God of Jacob;
Surely I will not come into the tabernacle of my house,
Nor go up into my bed;
I will not give sleep to mine eyes,
Or slumber to mine eyelids,
Until I find out a place for the LORD,
A habitation for the mighty God of Jacob.
Lo, we heard of it at Ephratah:
We found it in the fields of the wood.
We will go into his tabernacles:
We will worship at his footstool.
Arise, O LORD, into thy rest;
Thou, and the ark of thy strength.

Let thy priests be clothed with righteousness;
And let thy saints shout for joy.
For thy servant David's sake,
Turn not away the face of thine anointed.
The LORD hath sworn in truth unto David;
{ *He will not turn from it;*
{ *Of the fruit of thy body will I set upon thy throne.*
{ If thy children will keep my covenant
{ And my testimony that I shall teach them,
Their children shall also sit upon thy throne for evermore.
For the LORD hath chosen Zion ;
He hath desired it for his habitation.
This is my rest for ever:
Here will I dwell; for I have desired it.
I will abundantly bless her provision :
I will satisfy her poor with bread.
I will also clothe her priests with salvation:
And her saints shall shout aloud for joy.
There will I make the horn of David to bud :
I have ordained a lamp for mine anointed.
His enemies will I clothe with shame :
But upon himself shall his crown flourish.

PSALM CXXVII.

{ EXCEPT the LORD build the house,
{ They labor in vain that build it :
{ *Except the* LORD *keep the city,*
{ *The watchman waketh but in vain.*
{ It is vain for you to rise up early, to sit up late,
{ To eat the bread of sorrows:
For so he giveth his beloved sleep.
Lo, children are an heritage of the LORD :
And the fruit of the womb is his reward.
As arrows are in the hand of a mighty man,
So are children of the youth.
Happy is the man that hath his quiver full of them :
{ *They shall not be ashamed,*
{ *But they shall speak with the enemies in the gate.*

Psalm CXXXVIII.

I WILL praise thee with my whole heart:
Before the gods will I sing praise unto thee.
I will worship toward thy holy temple,
And praise thy name,
For thy loving-kindness and for thy truth:
For thou hast magnified thy word above all thy name.
In the day when I cried thou answeredst me,
And strengthenedst me with strength in my soul.
All the kings of the earth shall praise thee, O LORD,
When they hear the words of thy mouth.
Yea, they shall sing in the ways of the LORD:
For great is the glory of the LORD.
Though the LORD be high, yet hath he respect unto the lowly:
But the proud he knoweth afar off.
Though I walk in the midst of trouble, thou wilt revive me:
{ *Thou shalt stretch forth thine hand against the wrath of mine enemies,*
{ *And thy right hand shall save me.*
The LORD will perfect that which concerneth me:
{ *Thy mercy, O LORD, endureth for ever:*
{ *Forsake not the works of thine own hands.*

Lesson 25. (PAGE 57.)

Psalm CXLVI.

PRAISE ye the LORD.
Praise the LORD, O my soul.
While I live will I praise the LORD:
I will sing praises unto my God while I have any being.
Put not your trust in princes,
Nor in the son of man, in whom there is no help.
His breath goeth forth, he returneth to his earth;
In that very day his thoughts perish.
Happy is he that hath the God of Jacob for his help,
Whose hope is in the LORD his God:

Which made heaven, and earth, the sea, and all that therein is:
Which keepeth truth for ever:
Which executeth judgment for the oppressed:
Which giveth food to the hungry.
The LORD looseth the prisoners:
The LORD openeth the eyes of the blind:
The LORD raiseth up them that are bowed down:
The LORD loveth the righteous:
The LORD preserveth the strangers:
{ *He relieveth the fatherless and the widow:*
{ *But the way of the wicked he turneth upside down.*
The LORD shall reign forever,
Even thy God, O Zion, unto all generations.
PRAISE YE THE LORD.

PSALM CXLV.

I WILL extol thee, my God, O king;
And I will bless thy name for ever and ever.
Every day will I bless thee;
And I will praise thy name for ever and ever.
Great is the LORD, and greatly to be praised;
And his greatness is unsearchable.
One generation shall praise thy works to another,
And shall declare thy mighty acts.
I will speak of the glorious honor of thy majesty,
And of thy wondrous works.
And men shall speak of the might of thy terrible acts:
And I will declare thy greatness.
They shall abundantly utter the memory of thy great goodness,
And shall sing of thy righteousness.
The LORD is gracious, and full of compassion;
Slow to anger, and of great mercy.
The LORD is good to all:
And his tender mercies are over all his works.
All thy works shall praise thee, O LORD;
And thy saints shall bless thee.
They shall speak of the glory of thy kingdom,
And talk of thy power;
To make known to the sons of men his mighty acts,
And the glorious majesty of his kingdom.
Thy kingdom is an everlasting kingdom,
And thy dominion endureth throughout all generations.

The LORD upholdeth all that fall,
And raiseth up all those that be bowed down.
The eyes of all wait upon thee;
And thou givest them their meat in due season.
Thou openest thine hand,
And satisfiest the desire of every living thing.
The LORD is righteous in all his ways,
And holy in all his works.
The LORD is nigh unto all them that call upon him,
To all that call upon him in truth.
He will fulfil the desire of them that fear him,
He also will hear their cry, and will save them.
The LORD preserveth all them that love him:
But all the wicked will he destroy.
My mouth shall speak the praise of the LORD:
And let all flesh bless his holy name for ever and ever.

Lesson 26. (PAGE 59.)

PSALM CXLVII.

PRAISE ye the LORD: for it is good to sing praises unto our God;
For it is pleasant, and praise is comely.
The LORD doth build up Jerusalem:
He gathereth together the outcasts of Israel.
He healeth the broken in heart,
And bindeth up their wounds.
He telleth the number of the stars;
He calleth them all by their names.
Great is our LORD, and of great power:
His understanding is infinite.
The LORD lifteth up the meek:
He casteth the wicked down to the ground.
Sing unto the LORD with thanksgiving;
Sing praise upon the harp unto our God.
Who covereth the heaven with clouds,
{ *Who prepareth rain for the earth.*
{ *Who maketh grass to grow upon the mountains.*

He giveth to the beast his food,
  And to the young ravens which cry.
He delighteth not in the strength of the horse:
  He taketh not pleasure in the legs of a man.
The LORD taketh pleasure in them that fear him,
  In those that hope in his mercy.
Praise the LORD, O Jerusalem;
  Praise thy God, O Zion.
For he hath strengthened the bars of thy gates;
  He hath blessed thy children within thee.
He maketh peace in thy borders,
  And filleth thee with the finest of the wheat.
He sendeth forth his commandment upon earth:
  His word runneth very swiftly.
He giveth snow like wool:
  He scattereth the hoar frost like ashes.
He casteth forth his ice like morsels:
  Who can stand before his cold?
He sendeth out his word, and melteth them:
  He causeth his wind to blow, and the waters flow.
He showeth his word unto Jacob,
  His statutes and his judgments unto Israel.
He hath not dealt so with any nation:
  And as for his judgments, they have not known them.
PRAISE YE THE LORD.

PSALM CXLVIII.

PRAISE ye the LORD. Praise ye the LORD from the heavens:
  Praise him in the heights.
Praise ye him, all his angels:
  Praise ye him, all his hosts.
Praise ye him, sun and moon:
  Praise him, all ye stars of light.
Praise him, ye heavens of heavens,
  And ye waters that be above the heavens.
Let them praise the name of the LORD:
  For he commanded, and they were created.
He hath also stablished them for ever and ever:
  He hath made a decree which shall not pass.
Praise the LORD from the earth,
  Ye dragons, and all deeps:

Fire, and hail; snow, and vapor;
Stormy wind fulfilling his word:
Mountains, and all hills;
Fruitful trees, and all cedars:
Beasts, and all cattle;
Creeping things, and flying fowl:
Kings of the earth, and all people;
Princes, and all judges of the earth:
Both young men, and maidens:
Old men, and children:
Let them praise the name of the LORD:
For his name alone is excellent; his glory is above the earth and heaven.
He also exalteth the horn of his people,
The praise of all his saints;
Even of the children of Israel, a people near unto him.
Praise ye the LORD.

Lesson 27. (PAGE 61.)

PSALM CXXXV.

PRAISE ye the LORD. Praise ye the name of the LORD;
Praise him, O ye servants of the LORD.
Ye that stand in the house of the LORD,
In the courts of the house of our God,
Praise the LORD; for the LORD is good:
Sing praises unto his name; for it is pleasant.
For the LORD hath chosen Jacob unto himself,
And Israel for his peculiar treasure.
For I know that the LORD is great,
And that our LORD *is above all gods.*
Whatsoever the LORD pleased, that did he,
In heaven, and in earth, in the seas, and all deep places.
He causeth the vapors to ascend from the ends of the earth:
{ *He maketh lightnings for the rain;*
{ *He bringeth the wind out of his treasuries.*
Who smote the firstborn of Egypt,
Both of man and beast.

Who sent tokens and wonders into the midst of thee, O Egypt,
   Upon Pharaoh, and upon all his servants.
Who smote great nations, and slew mighty kings:
   { Sihon, king of the Amorites, and Og, king of Bashan,
   { And all the kingdoms of Canaan:
And gave their land for a heritage,
   A heritage unto Israel his people.
Thy name, O LORD, endureth for ever;
   And thy memorial, O LORD, throughout all generations.
For the LORD will judge his people,
   And he will repent himself concerning his servants.
The idols of the heathen are silver and gold,
   The work of men's hands.
They have mouths, but they speak not
   Eyes have they, but they see not;
They have ears, but they hear not;
   Neither is there any breath in their mouths.
They that make them are like unto them;
   So is every one that trusteth in them.
Bless the LORD, O house of Israel:
   Bless the LORD, O house of Aaron:
Bless the LORD, O house of Levi;
   Ye that fear the LORD, bless the LORD.
Blessed be the LORD out of Zion,
   Which dwelleth at Jerusalem.
PRAISE YE THE LORD.

Psalm CXLIX.

PRAISE ye the LORD.
   { Sing unto the LORD a new song,
   { And his praise in the congregation of saints.
Let Israel rejoice in him that made him:
   Let the children of Zion be joyful in their King.
Let them praise him in the dance:
   Let them sing praises unto him, with the timbrel and harp.
For the LORD taketh pleasure in his people:
   He will beautify the meek with salvation.
Let the saints be joyful in glory:
   Let them sing aloud upon their beds.
Let the high praises of God be in their mouth,
   And a two-edged sword in their hand!

To execute vengeance upon the heathen,
And punishments upon the people;
To bind their kings with chains,
And their nobles with fetters of iron;
To execute upon them the judgment written:
This honor have all his saints.
PRAISE YE THE LORD.

PSALM CL.

PRAISE ye the LORD. Praise God in his sanctuary:
Praise him in the firmament of his power.
Praise him for his mighty acts:
Praise him according to his excellent greatness.
Praise him with the sound of the trumpet:
Praise him with the psaltery and harp.
Praise him with the timbrel and dance:
Praise him with stringed instruments and organs.
Praise him upon the loud cymbals:
Praise him upon the high-sounding cymbals.
Let everything that hath breath praise the LORD.
PRAISE YE THE LORD.

Lesson 28. (PAGE 63.)

PSALM XLV.

MY heart is inditing a good matter :
{ *I speak of the things which I have made touching the king:*
{ *My tongue is the pen of a ready writer.*
Thou art fairer than the children of men : grace is poured into thy lips
Therefore God hath blessed thee for ever.
Gird thy sword upon thy thigh, O most Mighty,
With thy glory and thy majesty.
{ And in thy majesty ride prosperously,
{ Because of truth and meekness and righteousness ;
And thy right hand shall teach thee terrible things.
Thine arrows are sharp in the heart of the king's enemies ;
Whereby the people fall under thee.

Thy throne, O God, is for ever and ever:
   The sceptre of thy kingdom is a right sceptre.
Thou lovest righteousness, and hatest wickedness:
   Therefore God, thy God, hath anointed thee
   With the oil of gladness above thy fellows.
All thy garments smell of myrrh, and aloes, and cassia,
   Out of the ivory palaces, whereby they have made thee glad.
Kings' daughters were among thy honorable women:
   Upon thy right hand did stand the queen, in gold of Ophir.
Hearken, O daughter, and consider, and incline thine ear;
   Forget also thine own people, and thy father's house;
So shall the king greatly desire thy beauty:
   For he is thy LORD; *and worship thou him.*
And the daughter of Tyre shall be there with a gift;
   Even the rich among the people shall entreat thy favor.
The king's daughter is all glorious within:
   Her clothing is of wrought gold.
She shall be brought unto the king in raiment of needlework,
   The virgins her companions that follow her shall be brought unto thee.
With gladness and rejoicing shall they be brought:
   They shall enter into the king's palace.
Instead of thy fathers shall be thy children,
   Whom thou mayest make princes in all the earth.
I will make thy name to be remembered in all generations:
   Therefore shall the people praise thee, for ever and ever.

Psalm LXXII.

GIVE the king thy judgments, O God,
   And thy righteousness unto the king's son.
He shall judge thy people with righteousness,
   And thy poor with judgment.
The mountains shall bring peace to the people,
   And the little hills, by righteousness.
He shall judge the poor of the people,
   He shall save the children of the needy, and shall break in pieces the oppressor.
They shall fear thee as long as the sun and moon endure,
   Throughout all generations.
He shall come down like rain upon the mown grass:
   As showers that water the earth.
In his days shall the righteous flourish;
   And abundance of peace, so long as the moon endureth.

He shall have dominion also from sea to sea,
  And from the river unto the ends of the earth.
They that dwell in the wilderness shall bow before him;
  And his enemies shall lick the dust.
The kings of Tarshish and of the isles shall bring presents:
  The kings of Sheba and Seba shall offer gifts.
Yea, all kings shall fall down before him:
  All nations shall serve him.
For he shall deliver the needy when he crieth;
  The poor also, and him that hath no helper.
He shall spare the poor and needy,
  And shall save the souls of the needy.
He shall redeem their soul from deceit and violence:
  And precious shall their blood be in his sight.
And he shall live, and to him shall be given of the gold of Sheba:
  Prayer also shall be made for him continually; and daily shall he be praised.
There shall be a handful of corn in the earth, upon the top of the mountains;
  { *The fruit thereof shall shake like Lebanon:*
  { *And they of the city shall flourish like grass of the earth.*
His name shall endure for ever:
  { *His name shall be continued as long as the sun:*
  { *And men shall be blessed in him: all nations shall call him blessed.*
Blessed be the LORD God,
  The God of Israel, who only doeth wondrous things.
And blessed be his glorious name for ever:
  And let the whole earth be filled with his glory.
  AMEN, AND AMEN.

Lesson 29. (PAGE 65.)

PSALM II.

WHY do the heathen rage,
  And the people imagine a vain thing?
The kings of the earth set themselves,
  { *And the rulers take counsel together,*
  { *Against the Lord and against his anointed,*
Saying, Let us break their bands asunder,
  And cast away their cords from us.

He that sitteth in the heavens shall laugh:
    The LORD shall have them in derision.
Then shall he speak unto them in his wrath,
    And vex them in his sore displeasure.
Yet have I set my king
    Upon my holy hill of Zion.
I will declare the decree:
    { *The LORD hath said unto me, Thou art my Son;*
    { *This day have I begotten thee.*
Ask of me, and I shall give thee the heathen for thine inheritance,
    And the uttermost parts of the earth for thy possession.
Thou shalt break them with a rod of iron;
    Thou shalt dash them in pieces like a potter's vessel.
Be wise now therefore, O ye kings:
    Be instructed, ye judges of the earth.
Serve the LORD with fear,
    And rejoice with trembling.
Kiss the Son, lest he be angry, and ye perish from the way,
    When his wrath is kindled but a little.
BLESSED ARE ALL THEY THAT PUT THEIR TRUST IN HIM!

PSALM XXI.

THE king shall joy in thy strength, O LORD;
    And in thy salvation how greatly shall he rejoice!
Thou hast given him his heart's desire,
    And hast not withholden the request of his lips.
For thou preventest him with the blessings of goodness:
    Thou settest a crown of pure gold on his head.
He asked life of thee, and thou gavest it him,
    Even length of days for ever and ever.
His glory is great in thy salvation:
    Honor and majesty hast thou laid upon him.
For thou hast made him most blessed for ever:
    Thou hast made him exceeding glad with thy countenance.
For the king trusteth in the LORD,
    And through the mercy of the Most High he shall not be moved.
Thine hand shall find out all thine enemies:
    Thy right hand shall find out those that hate thee.
Thou shalt make them as a fiery oven in the time of thine anger:
    { *The LORD shall swallow them up in his wrath,*
    { *And the fire shall devour them.*

Their fruit shalt thou destroy from the earth,
  And their seed from among the children of men.
For they intended evil against thee :
  They imagined a mischievous device, which they are not able to perform.
Therefore shalt thou make them turn their back :
  When thou shalt make ready thine arrows upon thy strings, against the face of them.
Be thou exalted, LORD, in thine own strength ;
  So will we sing and praise thy power.

PSALM CX.

THE LORD said unto my Lord,
  { *Sit thou at my right hand,*
  { *Until I make thine enemies thy footstool.*
The LORD shall send the rod of thy strength out of Zion :
  Rule thou in the midst of thine enemies.
Thy people shall be willing in the day of thy power,
  { *In the beauties of holiness from the womb of the morning :*
  { *Thou hast the dew of thy youth.*
The LORD hath sworn, and will not repent,
  Thou art a priest for ever after the order of Melchizedek.
The Lord at thy right hand
  Shall strike through kings in the day of his wrath.
He shall judge among the heathen,
  { *He shall fill the places with the dead bodies ;*
  { *He shall wound the heads over many countries.*
He shall drink of the brook in the way :
  Therefore shall he lift up the head.

Lesson 30. (Page 68.)

Psalm LXVIII.

LET God arise, let his enemies be scattered:
Let them also that hate him flee before him.
As smoke is driven away, so drive them away:
As wax melteth before the fire, so let the wicked perish at the presence of God.
But let the righteous be glad; let them rejoice before God:
Yea, let them exceedingly rejoice.
Sing unto God, sing praises to his name:
{ *Extol him that rideth upon the heavens,*
{ *By his name JAH, and rejoice before him.*
A father of the fatherless, and a judge of the widows,
Is God in his holy habitation.
God setteth the solitary in families:
{ *He bringeth out those which are bound with chains:*
{ *But the rebellious dwell in a dry land.*
O God, when thou wentest forth before thy people,
When thou didst march through the wilderness;
The earth shook, the heavens also dropped at the presence of God:
Even Sinai itself was moved at the presence of God, the God of Israel.
Thou, O God, didst send a plentiful rain,
Whereby thou didst confirm thine inheritance, when it was weary.
Thy congregation hath dwelt therein:
Thou, O God, hast prepared of thy goodness for the poor.
The LORD gave the word:
Great was the company of those that published it.
Kings of armies did flee apace:
And she that tarried at home divided the spoil.
{ Though ye have lain among the pots,
{ *Yet shall ye be as the wings of a dove covered with silver,*
And her feathers with yellow gold.
When the Almighty scattered kings in it,
It was white as snow in Salmon.
The hill of God is as the hill of Bashan;
A high hill, as the hill of Bashan.
Why leap ye, ye high hills?
{ *This is the hill which God desireth to dwell in;*
{ *Yea, the LORD will dwell in it for ever.*

AS DEFENDER OF HIS PEOPLE.

The chariots of God are twenty thousand, even thousands of angels :
  The LORD *is among them, as in Sinai, in the holy place.*
Thou hast ascended on high, thou hast led captivity captive :
  { *Thou hast received gifts for men ;*
  { *Yea, for the rebellious also, that the* LORD *God might dwell among them.*
Blessed be the LORD, who daily loadeth us with benefits,
  Even the God of our salvation.
He that is our God is the God of Salvation ;
  And unto God the LORD *belong the issues from death.*
But God shall wound the head of his enemies,
  And the hairy scalp of such an one as goeth on still in his trespasses.
The LORD said, I will bring again from Bashan,
  I will bring my people again from the depths of the sea :
That thy foot may be dipped in the blood of thine enemies,
  And the tongue of thy dogs in the same.
They have seen thy goings, O God :
  Even the goings of my God, my King, in the sanctuary.
The singers went before, the players on instruments followed after :
  Among them were the damsels playing with timbrels.
Bless ye God in the congregations,
  Even the LORD, *from the fountain of Israel.*
There is little Benjamin with their ruler,
  { *The princes of Judah and their council,*
  { *The princes of Zebulun, and the princes of Naphtali.*
Thy God hath commanded thy strength :
  Strengthen, O God, that which thou hast wrought for us.
Because of thy temple at Jerusalem shall kings bring presents unto thee.
  Rebuke the company of spearmen, the multitude of the bulls, with the calves of the people,
Till every one submit himself with pieces of silver :
  Scatter thou the people that delight in war.
Princes shall come out of Egypt :
  Ethiopia shall soon stretch out her hands unto God.
Sing unto God, ye kingdoms of the earth ;
  Oh sing praises unto the LORD :
To him that rideth upon the heavens of heavens, which were of old ;
  Lo, he doth send out his voice, and that a mighty voice.
Ascribe ye strength unto God :
  His excellency is over Israel, and his strength is in the clouds.
O God, thou art terrible out of thy holy places :
  The God of Israel is he that giveth strength and power unto his people.
  BLESSED BE GOD.

Lesson 31. (Page 70.)

Psalm IV.

HEAR me when I call, O God of my righteousness:
 Thou hast enlarged me when I was in distress;
 Have mercy upon me and hear my prayer.
O ye sons of men, how long will ye turn my glory into shame?
 How long will ye love vanity, and seek after leasing?
But know that the LORD hath set apart him that is godly for himself:
 The LORD will hear when I call unto him.
Stand in awe, and sin not:
 Commune with your own heart upon your bed, and be still.
Offer the sacrifices of righteousness,
 And put your trust in the LORD.
There may be many that say, Who will show us any good?
 LORD, lift thou up the light of thy countenance upon us.
Thou hast put gladness in my heart,
 More than in the time that their corn and their wine increased.
I will both lay me down in peace and sleep:
 For thou, LORD, only makest me dwell in safety.

Psalm III.

LORD, how are they increased that trouble me!
 Many are they that rise up against me.
Many there be which say of my soul,
 There is no help for him in God.
But thou, O LORD, art a shield for me;
 My glory, and the lifter up of mine head.
I cried unto the LORD with my voice,
 And he heard me out of his holy hill.
I laid me down and slept;
 I awaked; for the LORD sustained me.
I will not be afraid of ten thousands of people,
 That have set themselves against me round about.
Arise, O LORD; save me, O my God:
 For thou hast smitten all mine enemies upon the cheek bone;
 Thou hast broken the teeth of the ungodly.
Salvation belongeth unto the LORD;
 Thy blessing is upon thy people.

Psalm XX.

THE LORD hear thee in the day of trouble;
The name of the God of Jacob defend thee;
Send thee help from the sanctuary,
And strengthen thee out of Zion;
Remember all thy offerings,
And accept thy burnt sacrifice;
Grant thee according to thine own heart,
And fulfil all thy counsel.
{ We will rejoice in thy salvation,
{ And in the name of our God we will set up our banners:
The LORD fulfil all thy petitions.
Now know I that the LORD saveth his anointed;
{ *He will hear him from his holy heaven,*
{ *With the saving strength of his right hand.*
Some trust in chariots, and some in horses:
But we will remember the name of the LORD our God.
They are brought down and fallen:
But we are risen, and stand upright.
Save, LORD:
Let the king hear us when we call.

Lesson 32. (Page 71.)

Psalm XVIII : 1—35.

I WILL love thee, O LORD, my strength.
The LORD is my rock, and my fortress, and my deliverer;
My God, my strength, in whom I will trust;
My buckler, and the horn of my salvation, and my high tower.
I will call upon the LORD, who is worthy to be praised:
So shall I be saved from mine enemies.
The sorrows of death compassed me,
And the floods of ungodly men made me afraid.
The sorrows of hell compassed me about:
The snares of death prevented me.

In my distress I called upon the LORD,
  And cried unto my God:
He heard my voice out of his temple,
  And my cry came before him, even into his ears.
Then the earth shook and trembled;
  { *The foundations also of the hills moved*
  { *And were shaken, because he was wroth.*
There went up a smoke out of his nostrils,
  And fire out of his mouth devoured: coals were kindled by it.
He bowed the heavens also, and came down:
  And darkness was under his feet,
And he rode upon a cherub, and did fly:
  Yea, he did fly upon the wings of the wind.
He made darkness his secret place;
  His pavilion round about him were dark waters, and thick clouds of the skies.
At the brightness that was before him his thick clouds passed,
  Hail stones and coals of fire.
The LORD also thundered in the heavens,
  And the Highest gave his voice; hail stones and coals of fire.
Yea, he sent out his arrows, and scattered them;
  And he shot out lightnings, and discomfited them.
Then the channels of waters were seen,
  And the foundations of the world were discovered,
At thy rebuke, O LORD,
  At the blast of the breath of thy nostrils.
He sent from above, he took me,
  He drew me out of many waters.
He delivered me from my strong enemy,
  And from them which hated me; for they were too strong for me.
They prevented me in the day of my calamity:
  But the LORD was my stay.
He brought me forth also into a large place;
  He delivered me, because he delighted in me.
The LORD rewarded me according to my righteousness:
  According to the cleanness of my hands hath he recompensed me.
For I have kept the ways of the LORD,
  And have not wickedly departed from my God.
For all his judgments were before me,
  And I did not put away his statutes from me.
I was also upright before him,
  And I kept myself from mine iniquity.
Therefore hath the LORD recompensed me according to my righteousness,
  According to the cleanness of my hands in his eyesight.

With the merciful thou wilt show thyself merciful ;
  With an upright man thou wilt show thyself upright.
With the pure thou wilt show thyself pure ;
  And with the froward thou wilt show thyself froward.
For thou wilt save the afflicted people ;
  But will bring down high looks.
For thou wilt light my candle ;
  The LORD my God will enlighten my darkness.
For by thee I have run through a troop ;
  And by my God have I leaped over a wall.
As for God, his way is perfect :
  { *The word of the LORD is tried :*
  { *He is a buckler to all those that trust in him.*
For who is God save the LORD ?
  Or who is a rock save our God?
It is God that girdeth me with strength,
  And maketh my way perfect.
He maketh my feet like hind's feet,
  And setteth me upon my high places.
He teacheth my hands to war,
  So that a bow of steel is broken by mine arms.
Thou hast also given me the shield of thy salvation :
  { *And thy right hand hath holden me up,*
  { *And thy gentleness hath made me great.*

Lesson 33. (PAGE 73.)

PSALM XVII.

HEAR the right, O LORD, attend unto my cry ;
  Give ear unto my prayer, that goeth not out of feigned lips.
Let my sentence come forth from thy presence ;
  Let thine eyes behold the things that are equal.
Thou hast proved mine heart ; thou hast visited me in the night ;
  { *Thou hast tried me, and shalt find nothing :*
  { *I am purposed that my mouth shall not transgress.*
Concerning the works of men,
  By the word of thy lips I have kept me from the paths of the destroyer.

Hold up my goings in thy paths,
  That my footsteps slip not.
I have called upon thee, for thou wilt hear me, O God:
  Incline thine ear unto me, and hear my speech.
Show thy marvellous loving-kindness,
  { *O thou that savest by thy right hand them which put their trust in thee,*
  { *From those that rise up against them.*
Keep me as the apple of the eye;
  Hide me under the shadow of thy wings.
From the wicked that oppress me,
  From my deadly enemies, who compass me about.
They are enclosed in their own fat:
  With their mouth they speak proudly.
They have now compassed us in our steps:
  They have set their eyes bowing down to the earth;
Like as a lion that is greedy of his prey,
  And as it were a young lion lurking in secret places.
Arise, O LORD, disappoint him, cast him down;
  Deliver my soul from the wicked, which is thy sword:
From men which are thy hand, O LORD, from men of the world,
  { *Which have their portion in this life, and whose belly thou fillest with thy*
  {   *hid treasure:*
  { *They are full of children, and leave the rest of their substance to their babes.*
As for me, I will behold thy face in righteousness:
  I shall be satisfied, when I awake, with thy likeness.

Psalm CXV.

NOT unto us, O LORD, not unto us, but unto thy name give glory,
  For thy mercy, and for thy truth's sake.
Wherefore should the heathen say,
  Where is now their God?
But our God is in the heavens:
  He hath done whatsoever he hath pleased.
Their idols are silver and gold,
  The work of men's hands.
They have mouths, but they speak not:
  Eyes have they, but they see not:
They have ears, but they hear not:
  Noses have they, but they smell not:
They have hands, but they handle not:
  Feet have they, but they walk not: neither speak they through their throat.

They that make them are like unto them;
So is every one that trusteth in them.
O Israel, trust thou in the LORD:
He is their help and their shield.
O house of Aaron, trust in the LORD:
He is their help and their shield.
Ye that fear the LORD, trust in the LORD:
He is their help and their shield.
The LORD hath been mindful of us: he will bless us;
He will bless the house of Israel; he will bless the house of Aaron.
He will bless them that fear the LORD:
Both small and great.
The LORD shall increase you more and more,
You and your children.
Ye are blessed of the LORD,
Which made heaven and earth.
The heaven, even the heavens, are the LORD's:
But the earth hath he given to the children of men.
The dead praise not the LORD,
Neither any that go down into silence.
But we will bless the LORD,
From this time forth, and for evermore.
PRAISE THE LORD.

Lesson 34. (PAGE 75.)

FROM PSALM XXXVII.

FRET not thyself because of evil-doers,
Neither be thou envious against the workers of iniquity.
For they shall soon be cut down like the grass,
And wither as the green herb.
Trust in the LORD, and do good;
So shalt thou dwell in the land, and verily thou shalt be fed.
Delight thyself also in the LORD;
And he shall give thee the desires of thine heart.
Commit thy way unto the LORD;
Trust also in him; and he shall bring it to pass.

And he shall bring forth thy righteousness as the light,
And thy judgment as the noonday.
Rest in the LORD, and wait patiently for him :
Fret not thyself because of him who prospereth in his way,
Because of the man who bringeth wicked devices to pass.
Cease from anger, and forsake wrath :
Fret not thyself in any wise to do evil.
For evil-doers shall be cut off:
But those that wait upon the LORD, they shall inherit the earth.
For yet a little while, and the wicked shall not be :
Yea, thou shalt diligently consider his place, and it shall not be.
But the meek shall inherit the earth :
And shall delight themselves in the abundance of peace.
A little that a righteous man hath
Is better than the riches of many wicked.
For the arms of the wicked shall be broken :
But the LORD upholdeth the righteous.
The LORD knoweth the days of the upright :
And their inheritance shall be for ever.
They shall not be ashamed in the evil time :
And in the days of famine they shall be satisfied.
For such as be blessed of him shall inherit the earth ;
And they that be cursed of him shall be cut off.
The steps of a good man are ordered by the LORD :
And he delighteth in his way.
Though he fall, he shall not be utterly cast down :
For the LORD upholdeth him with his hand.
I have been young, and now am old :
Yet have I not seen the righteous forsaken, nor his seed begging bread.
He is ever merciful, and lendeth ;
And his seed is blessed.
Depart from evil, and do good ;
And dwell for evermore.
For the LORD loveth judgment,
And forsaketh not his saints ;
They are preserved forever:
But the seed of the wicked shall be cut off.
The righteous shall inherit the land,
And dwell therein forever.
The mouth of the righteous speaketh wisdom,
And his tongue talketh of judgment.
The law of his God is in his heart ;
None of his steps shall slide.

The wicked watcheth the righteous,
   And seeketh to slay him.
The LORD will not leave him in his hand,
   Nor condemn him when he is judged.
{ Wait on the LORD and keep his way,
{ And he shall exalt thee to inherit the land :
   When the wicked are cut off, thou shalt see it.
I have seen the wicked in great power,
   And spreading himself like a green bay tree.
Yet he passed away, and, lo, he was not :
   Yea, I sought him, but he could not be found.
Mark the perfect man, and behold the upright :
   For the end of that man is peace.
But the transgressors shall be destroyed together :
   The end of the wicked shall be cut off.
But the salvation of the righteous is of the LORD :
   He is their strength in the time of trouble.
And the LORD shall help them, and deliver them :
{ *He shall deliver them from the wicked,*
{ *And save them, because they trust in him.*

Lesson 35. (PAGE 77.)

PSALM LXVII.

GOD be merciful unto us, and bless us :
   And cause his face to shine upon us.
That thy way may be known upon earth,
   Thy saving health among all nations.
Let the people praise thee, O God ;
   Let all the people praise thee.
Oh let the nations be glad and sing for joy :
{ *For thou shalt judge the people righteously,*
{ *And govern the nations upon earth.*
Let the people praise thee, O God,
   Let all the people praise thee.
Then shall the earth yield her increase ;
   And God, even our own God, shall bless us.
God shall bless us ;
   And all the ends of the earth shall fear him.

Psalm LXXV.

UNTO thee, O God, do we give thanks,
    Unto thee do we give thanks:
    For that thy name is near thy wondrous works declare.
When I shall receive the congregation,
    I will judge uprightly.
The earth and all the inhabitants thereof are dissolved:
    I bear up the pillars of it.
I said unto the fools, Deal not foolishly:
    And to the wicked, Lift not up the horn:
    Lift not up your horn on high: speak not with a stiff neck.
For promotion cometh neither from the east,
    Nor from the west, nor from the south.
But God is the judge:
    He putteth down one, and setteth up another.
For in the hand of the LORD there is a cup,
    And the wine is red; it is full of mixture;
And he poureth out of the same:
    But the dregs thereof, all the wicked of the earth shall wring them out, and drink them.
But I will declare for ever;
    I will sing praises to the God of Jacob.
All the horns of the wicked also will I cut off:
    But the horn of the righteous shall be exalted.

Psalm LXXVI.

IN Judah is God known:
    His name is great in Israel.
In Salem also is his tabernacle,
    And his dwelling-place in Zion.
There brake he the arrows of the bow,
    The shield, and the sword, and the battle.
Thou art more glorious and excellent than the mountains of prey.
    The stouthearted are spoiled,
They have slept their sleep:
    And none of the men of might have found their hands.
At thy rebuke, O God of Jacob,
    Both the chariot and horse are cast into a dead sleep.
Thou, even thou, art to be feared:
    And who may stand in thy sight when once thou art angry?

Thou didst cause judgment to be heard from heaven;
  The earth feared, and was still,
When God arose to judgment,
  To save all the meek of the earth.
Surely the wrath of man shall praise thee:
  The remainder of wrath shalt thou restrain.
Vow, and pay unto the LORD your God:
  Let all that be round about him bring presents unto him that ought to be feared.
He shall cut off the spirit of princes:
  He is terrible to the kings of the earth.

Lesson 36. (PAGE 79.)

PSALM LXXVII.

I CRIED unto God with my voice,
  Even unto God with my voice; and he gave ear unto me.
In the day of my trouble I sought the Lord:
  My sore ran in the night, and ceased not: my soul refused to be comforted.
I remembered God, and was troubled:
  I complained, and my spirit was overwhelmed.
Thou holdest mine eyes waking:
  I am so troubled that I cannot speak.
I have considered the days of old,
  The years of ancient times.
I call to remembrance my song in the night:
  I commune with mine own heart: and my spirit made diligent search.
Will the Lord cast off for ever?
  And will he be favorable no more?
Is his mercy clean gone for ever?
  Doth his promise fail for evermore?
Hath God forgotten to be gracious?
  Hath he in anger shut up his tender mercies?
And I said, This is my infirmity:
  But I will remember the years of the right hand of the Most High.
I will remember the works of the LORD:
  Surely I will remember thy wonders of old.

I will meditate also of all thy work,
  And talk of thy doings.
Thy way, O God, is in the sanctuary:
  Who is so great a God as our God?
Thou art the God that doest wonders:
  Thou hast declared thy strength among the people.
Thou hast with thine arm redeemed thy people,
  The sons of Jacob and Joseph.
The waters saw thee, O God, the waters saw thee;
  They were afraid: the depths also were troubled.
The clouds poured out water:
  The skies sent out a sound: thine arrows also went abroad.
The voice of thy thunder was in the heaven:
  The lightnings lightened the world: the earth trembled and shook.
Thy way is in the sea,
  And thy path in the great waters, and thy footsteps are not known.
Thou leddest thy people like a flock,
  By the hand of Moses and Aaron.

Psalm LXXX.

GIVE ear, O Shepherd of Israel, thou that leadest Joseph like a flock;
  Thou that dwellest between the cherubim, shine forth.
Before Ephraim and Benjamin and Manasseh stir up thy strength,
  And come, and save us.
Turn us again, O God,
  And cause thy face to shine; and we shall be saved.
O Lord God of hosts,
  How long wilt thou be angry against the prayer of thy people?
Thou feedest them with the bread of tears;
  And givest them tears to drink in great measure.
Thou makest us a strife unto our neighbors:
  And our enemies laugh among themselves.
Turn us again, O God of hosts,
  And cause thy face to shine; and we shall be saved.
Thou hast brought a vine out of Egypt:
  Thou hast cast out the heathen, and planted it.
Thou preparedst room before it,
  And didst cause it to take deep root, and it filled the land.
The hills were covered with the shadow of it,
  And the boughs thereof were like the goodly cedars.
She sent out her boughs unto the sea,
  And her branches unto the river.

Why hast thou then broken down her hedges,
So that all they which pass by the way do pluck her?
The boar out of the wood doth waste it,
And the wild beast of the field doth devour it.
Return, we beseech thee, O God of hosts:
Look down from heaven, and behold, and visit this vine;
And the vineyard which thy right hand hath planted,
And the branch that thou madest strong for thyself.
It is burned with fire, it is cut down:
They perish at the rebuke of thy countenance.
Let thy hand be upon the man of thy right hand,
Upon the son of man whom thou madest strong for thyself.
So will not we go back from thee:
Quicken us, and we will call upon thy name.
Turn us again, O LORD God of hosts,
Cause thy face to shine; and we shall be saved.

Lesson 37. (Page 81.)

Psalm LXXXIX : 1—34.

I WILL sing of the mercies of the LORD for ever:
With my mouth will I make known thy faithfulness to all generations.
For I have said, Mercy shall be built up for ever:
Thy faithfulness shalt thou establish in the very heavens.
I have made a covenant with my chosen,
I have sworn unto David my servant,
Thy seed will I establish for ever,
And build up thy throne to all generations.
And the heavens shall praise thy wonders, O LORD:
Thy faithfulness also in the congregation of the saints.
For who in the heavens can be compared unto the LORD:
Who among the sons of the mighty can be likened unto the LORD?
God is greatly to be feared in the assembly of the saints,
And to be had in reverence of all them that are about him.
O LORD God of hosts, who is a strong LORD like unto thee?
Or to thy faithfulness round about thee?
Thou rulest the raging of the sea:
When the waves thereof arise, thou stillest them.

Thou hast broken Rahab in pieces, as one that is slain;
  Thou hast scattered thine enemies with thy strong arm.
The heavens are thine, the earth also is thine:
  As for the world and the fulness thereof, thou hast founded them.
The north and the south, thou hast created them:
  Tabor and Hermon shall rejoice in thy name.
Thou hast a mighty arm:
  Strong is thy hand, and high is thy right hand.
Justice and judgment are the habitation of thy throne:
  Mercy and truth shall go before thy face.
Blessed is the people that know the joyful sound:
  They shall walk, O LORD, *in the light of thy countenance.*
In thy name shall they rejoice all the day:
  And in thy righteousness shall they be exalted.
For thou art the glory of their strength:
  And in thy favor our horn shall be exalted.
For the LORD is our defence;
  And the Holy One of Israel is our king.
Then thou spakest in vision to thy holy one, and saidst,
  { *I have laid help upon one that is mighty;*
  { *I have exalted one chosen out of the people.*
I have found David my servant;
  With my holy oil have I anointed him:
With whom my hand shall be established:
  Mine arm also shall strengthen him.
The enemy shall not exact upon him:
  Nor the son of wickedness afflict him.
And I will beat down his foes before his face,
  And plague them that hate him.
But my faithfulness and my mercy shall be with him:
  And in my name shall his horn be exalted.
I will set his hand also in the sea,
  And his right hand in the rivers.
He shall cry unto me, Thou art my father,
  My God, and the rock of my salvation.
Also I will make him my firstborn,
  Higher than the kings of the earth.
My mercy will I keep for him for evermore,
  And my covenant shall stand fast with him.
His seed also will I make to endure for ever,
  And his throne as the days of heaven.
If his children forsake my law,
  And walk not in my judgments;

If they break my statutes,
> And keep not my commandments;

Then will I visit their transgression with the rod,
> And their iniquity with stripes.

Nevertheless my loving-kindness will I not utterly take from him,
> Nor suffer my faithfulness to fail.

My covenant will I not break,
> Nor alter the thing that is gone out of my lips.

Lesson 38. (Page 83.)

Psalm XC.

LORD, thou hast been our dwelling-place,
> In all generations.

Before the mountains were brought forth,
Or ever thou hadst formed the earth and the world,
> Even from everlasting to everlasting, thou art God.

Thou turnest man to destruction;
> And sayest, Return, ye children of men.

For a thousand years in thy sight are but as yesterday when it is past,
> And as a watch in the night.

Thou carriest them away as with a flood; they are as a sleep:
> In the morning they are like grass which groweth up;

In the morning it flourisheth, and groweth up;
> In the evening it is cut down, and withereth.

For we are consumed by thine anger,
> And by thy wrath are we troubled.

Thou hast set our iniquities before thee,
> Our secret sins in the light of thy countenance.

For all our days are passed away in thy wrath:
> We spend our years as a tale that is told.

The days of our years are threescore years and ten:
> And if by reason of strength they be fourscore years,

Yet is their strength labor and sorrow;
> For it is soon cut off, and we fly away.

Who knoweth the power of thine anger?
> Even according to thy fear, so is thy wrath.

So teach us to number our days,
    That we may apply our hearts unto wisdom.
Return, O Lord, how long?
    And let it repent thee concerning thy servants.
O satisfy us early with thy mercy:
    That we may rejoice and be glad all our days.
Make us glad according to the days wherein thou hast afflicted us,
    And the years wherein we have seen evil.
Let thy work appear unto thy servants,
    And thy glory unto their children.
And let the beauty of the Lord our God be upon us:
    { *And establish thou the work of our hands upon us;*
    { *Yea, the work of our hands establish thou it.*

Psalm XCI.

HE that dwelleth in the secret place of the Most High
    Shall abide under the shadow of the Almighty.
I will say of the Lord, He is my refuge and my fortress:
    My God; in him will I trust.
Surely he shall deliver thee from the snare of the fowler,
    And from the noisome pestilence.
He shall cover thee with his feathers, and under his wings shalt thou trust:
    His truth shall be thy shield and buckler.
Thou shalt not be afraid for the terror by night;
    Nor for the arrow that flieth by day;
Nor for the pestilence that walketh in darkness:
    Nor for the destruction that wasteth at noonday.
A thousand shall fall at thy side, and ten thousand at thy right hand;
    But it shall not come nigh thee.
Only with thine eyes shalt thou behold,
    And see the reward of the wicked.
Because thou hast made the Lord, which is my refuge,
    Even the Most High, thy habitation;
There shall no evil befall thee,
    Neither shall any plague come nigh thy dwelling.
For he shall give his angels charge over thee,
    To keep thee in all thy ways.
They shall bear thee up in their hands,
    Lest thou dash thy foot against a stone.
Thou shalt tread upon the lion and adder:
    The young lion, and the dragon, shalt thou trample under feet.

Because he hath set his love upon me, therefore will I deliver him:
I will set him on high, because he hath known my name.
He shall call upon me, and I will answer him:
I will be with him in trouble; I will deliver him and honor him.
With long life will I satisfy him,
And show him my salvation.

Lesson 39. (Page 85.)

Psalm CXLIV.

BLESSED be the LORD my strength,
Which teacheth my hands to war, and my fingers to fight.
My goodness, and my fortress;
My high tower, and my deliverer;
My shield, and he in whom I trust;
Who subdueth my people under me.
LORD, what is man, that thou takest knowledge of him!
Or the son of man, that thou makest account of him!
Man is like to vanity:
His days are as a shadow that passeth away.
Bow thy heavens, O LORD, and come down:
Touch the mountains, and they shall smoke.
Cast forth lightnings, and scatter them:
Shoot out thine arrows, and destroy them.
Send thine hand from above;
Rid me, and deliver me out of great waters,
From the hand of strange children;
{ *Whose mouth speaketh vanity,*
{ *And their right hand is a right hand of falsehood.*
I will sing a new song unto thee, O God:
Upon a psaltery and an instrument of ten strings will I sing praises unto thee.
It is he that giveth salvation unto kings:
Who delivereth David his servant from the hurtful sword.
Rid me, and deliver me from the hand of strange children,
{ *Whose mouth speaketh vanity,*
{ *And their right hand is a right hand of falsehood:*

That our sons may be as plants grown up in their youth;
That our daughters may be as corner stones, polished after the similitude of a palace;
That our garners may be full, affording all manner of store;
That our sheep may bring forth thousands and ten thousands in our streets:
That our oxen may be strong to labor; that there be no breaking in, nor going out:
That there be no complaining in our streets.
Happy is that people, that is in such a case:
Yea, happy is that people whose God is the LORD.

Psalm IX.

I WILL praise thee, O LORD, with my whole heart;
I will show forth all thy marvellous works.
I will be glad and rejoice in thee:
I will sing praise to thy name, O thou Most High.
When mine enemies are turned back,
They shall fall and perish at thy presence.
For thou hast maintained my right and my cause;
Thou satest in the throne judging right.
Thou hast rebuked the heathen, thou hast destroyed the wicked,
Thou hast put out their name for ever and ever.
O thou enemy, destructions are come to a perpetual end:
And thou hast destroyed cities; their memorial is perished with them.
But the LORD shall endure for ever;
He hath prepared his throne for judgment.
And he shall judge the world in righteousness,
He shall minister judgment to the people in uprightness.
The LORD also will be a refuge for the oppressed,
A refuge in times of trouble.
And they that know thy name will put their trust in thee:
For thou, LORD, hast not forsaken them that seek thee.
Sing praises to the LORD, which dwelleth in Zion:
Declare among the people his doings.
When he maketh inquisition for blood, he remembereth them:
He forgetteth not the cry of the humble.
Have mercy upon me, O LORD;
{ *Consider my trouble which I suffer of them that hate me,*
{ *Thou that liftest me up from the gates of death:*
That I may show forth all thy praise in the gates of the daughter of Zion:
I will rejoice in thy salvation.

The heathen are sunk down in the pit that they made:
In the net which they hid is their own foot taken.
The LORD is known by the judgment which he executeth:
The wicked is snared in the work of his own hands.
The wicked shall be turned into hell,
And all the nations that forget God.
For the needy shall not always be forgotten:
The expectation of the poor shall not perish for ever.
Arise, O LORD; let not man prevail:
Let the heathen be judged in thy sight.
Put them in fear, O LORD:
That the nations may know themselves to be but men.

Lesson 40. (PAGE 87.)

PSALM LXIV.

HEAR my voice, O God, in my prayer:
Preserve my life from fear of the enemy.
Hide me from the secret counsel of the wicked;
From the insurrection of the workers of iniquity:
Who whet their tongue like a sword,
And bend their bows to shoot their arrows, even bitter words:
That they may shoot in secret at the perfect:
Suddenly do they shoot at him, and fear not.
They encourage themselves in an evil matter;
They commune of laying snares privily; they say, Who shall see them?
They search out iniquities; they accomplish a diligent search:
Both the inward thought of every one of them, and the heart is deep.
But God shall shoot at them with an arrow;
Suddenly shall they be wounded.
So they shall make their own tongue to fall upon themselves:
All that see them shall flee away.
And all men shall fear, and shall declare the work of God;
For they shall wisely consider of his doing.
The righteous shall be glad in the LORD, and shall trust in him;
And all the upright in heart shall glory.

Psalm LXII.

TRULY my soul waiteth upon God:
 From him cometh my salvation.
He only is my rock and my salvation;
 He is my defence; I shall not be greatly moved.
How long will ye imagine mischief against a man?
 { *Ye shall be slain all of you;*
 { *As a bowing wall shall ye be, and as a tottering fence.*
They only consult to cast him down from his excellency:
 They delight in lies: they bless with their mouth, but they curse inwardly.
My soul, wait thou only upon God;
 For my expectation is from him.
He only is my rock and my salvation:
 He is my defence; I shall not be moved.
In God is my salvation and my glory:
 The rock of my strength, and my refuge, is in God.
Trust in him at all times;
 Ye people, pour out your heart before him: God is a refuge for us.
Surely men of low degree are vanity, and men of high degree are a lie:
 To be laid in the balance, they are altogether lighter than vanity.
Trust not in oppression, and become not vain in robbery
 If riches increase, set not your heart upon them.
God hath spoken once; twice have I heard this;
 That power belongeth unto God.
Also unto thee, O LORD, belongeth mercy:
 For thou renderest to every man according to his work.

Psalm CXXIV.

IF it had not been the LORD who was on our side,
 Now may Israel say;
If it had not been the LORD who was on our side,
 When men rose up against us:
Then they had swallowed us up quick,
 When their wrath was kindled against us:
Then the waters had overwhelmed us,
 { *The stream had gone over our soul:*
 { *Then the proud waters had gone over our soul.*
Blessed be the LORD,
 Who hath not given us as a prey to their teeth.

Our soul is escaped as a bird out of the snare of the fowlers:
The snare is broken, and we are escaped.
Our help is in the name of the Lord,
Who made heaven and earth.

Lesson 41. (Page 89.)

Psalm XXV.

UNTO thee, O Lord, do I lift up my soul;
O my God, I trust in thee:
Let me not be ashamed,
Let not mine enemies triumph over me.
Yea, let none that wait on thee be ashamed:
Let them be ashamed which transgress without cause.
Show me thy ways, O Lord;
Teach me thy paths.
Lead me in thy truth, and teach me:
For thou art the God of my salvation; on thee do I wait all the day.
Remember, O Lord, thy tender mercies and thy loving-kindnesses;
For they have been ever of old.
Remember not the sins of my youth, nor my transgressions:
According to thy mercy remember thou me for thy goodness' sake, O Lord.
Good and upright is the Lord:
Therefore will he teach sinners in the way.
The meek will he guide in judgment:
And the meek will he teach his way.
All the paths of the Lord are mercy and truth
Unto such as keep his covenant and his testimonies.
For thy name's sake, O Lord, pardon mine iniquity;
For it is great.
What man is he that feareth the Lord?
Him shall he teach in the way that he shall choose.
His soul shall dwell at ease;
And his seed shall inherit the earth.
The secret of the Lord is with them that fear him;
And he will show them his covenant.
Mine eyes are ever toward the Lord;
For he shall pluck my feet out of the net.

Turn thee unto me, and have mercy upon me ;
   For I am desolate and afflicted.
The troubles of my heart are enlarged :
   O bring thou me out of my distresses.
Look upon mine affliction and my pain ;
   And forgive all my sins.
Consider mine enemies; for they are many ;
   And they hate me with cruel hatred.
O keep my soul, and deliver me :
   Let me not be ashamed ; for I put my trust in thee.
Let integrity and uprightness preserve me ; for I wait on thee.
   Redeem Israel, O God, out of all his troubles.

Psalm XXXVI.

THE transgression of the wicked saith within my heart,
   That there is no fear of God before his eyes.
For he flattereth himself in his own eyes,
   Until his iniquity be found to be hateful.
The words of his mouth are iniquity and deceit :
   He hath left off to be wise, and to do good.
He deviseth mischief upon his bed ;
   He setteth himself in a way that is not good ; he abhorreth not evil.
Thy mercy, O Lord, is in the heavens ;
   And thy faithfulness reacheth unto the clouds.
Thy righteousness is like the great mountains :
   Thy judgments are a great deep : O Lord, thou preservest man and beast.
How excellent is thy loving-kindness, O God !
   Therefore the children of men put their trust under the shadow of thy wings.
They shall be abundantly satisfied with the fatness of thy house ;
   And thou shalt make them drink of the river of thy pleasures.
For with thee is the fountain of life ;
   In thy light shall we see light.
Oh continue thy loving-kindness unto them that know thee ;
   And thy righteousness to the upright in heart.
Let not the foot of pride come against me,
   And let not the hand of the wicked remove me.
There are the workers of iniquity fallen :
   They are cast down, and shall not be able to rise.

Lesson 42. (Page 91.)

Psalm XLI.

BLESSED is he that considereth the poor:
The LORD will deliver him in time of trouble.
The LORD will preserve him, and keep him alive;
  And he shall be blessed upon the earth:
  And thou wilt not deliver him unto the will of his enemies.
The LORD will strengthen him upon the bed of languishing:
Thou wilt make all his bed in his sickness.
I said, LORD, be merciful unto me:
Heal my soul; for I have sinned against thee.
Mine enemies speak evil of me,
When shall he die, and his name perish?
And if he come to see me, he speaketh vanity:
His heart gathereth iniquity to itself; when he goeth abroad, he telleth it.
All that hate me whisper together against me:
Against me do they devise my hurt.
An evil disease, say they, cleaveth fast unto him:
And now that he lieth he shall rise up no more.
Yea, mine own familiar friend, in whom I trusted,
Which did eat of my bread, hath lifted up his heel against me.
But thou, O LORD, be merciful unto me, and raise me up,
That I may requite them.
By this I know that thou favorest me,
Because mine enemy doth not triumph over me.
And as for me, thou upholdest me in mine integrity,
And settest me before thy face forever.
Blessed be the LORD God of Israel
From everlasting, and to everlasting. Amen, and Amen.

Psalm XXXII.

BLESSED is he whose transgression is forgiven,
Whose sin is covered.
Blessed is the man unto whom the LORD imputeth not iniquity,
And in whose spirit there is no guile.
When I kept silence, my bones waxed old
Through my roaring all the day long.

For day and night thy hand was heavy upon me:
  My moisture is turned into the drought of summer.
I acknowledged my sin unto thee, and mine iniquity have I not hid.
  I said, I will confess my transgressions unto the LORD;
  And thou forgavest the iniquity of my sin.
For this shall every one that is godly pray unto thee
In a time when thou mayest be found:
  Surely in the floods of great waters they shall not come nigh unto him.
Thou art my hiding place;
  Thou shalt preserve me from trouble;
  Thou shalt compass me about with songs of deliverance.
I will instruct thee, and teach thee in the way which thou shalt go:
  I will guide thee with mine eye.
Be ye not as the horse, or as the mule, which have no understanding:
  Whose mouth must be held in with bit and bridle,
  Lest they come near unto thee.
Many sorrows shall be to the wicked:
  But he that trusteth in the LORD, *mercy shall compass him about.*
Be glad in the LORD, and rejoice, ye righteous:
  And shout for joy, all ye that are upright in heart.

PSALM LXI.

HEAR my cry, O God;
  Attend unto my prayer.
From the end of the earth will I cry unto thee, when my heart is overwhelmed:
  Lead me to the rock that is higher than I.
For thou hast been a shelter for me,
  And a strong tower from the enemy.
I will abide in thy tabernacle for ever:
  I will trust in the covert of thy wings.
For thou, O God, hast heard my vows:
  Thou hast given me the heritage of those that fear thy name.
Thou wilt prolong the king's life:
  And his years as many generations.
He shall abide before God for ever:
  Oh prepare mercy and truth, which may preserve him.
So will I sing praise unto thy name for ever,
  That I may daily perform my vows.

Lesson 43. (Page 93.)

From Psalm XLIV.

WE have heard with our ears, O God, our fathers have told us,
What work thou didst in their days, in the times of old.
How thou didst drive out the heathen with thy hand, and plantedst them.
How thou didst afflict the people, and cast them out.
For they got not the land in possession by their own sword,
Neither did their own arm save them:
But thy right hand, and thine arm, and the light of thy countenance,
Because thou hadst a favor unto them.
Thou art my King, O God:
Command deliverances for Jacob.
Through thee will we push down our enemies:
Through thy name will we tread them under that rise up against us.
For I will not trust in my bow,
Neither shall my sword save me.
But thou hast saved us from our enemies,
And hast put them to shame that hated us.
In God we boast all the day long,
And praise thy name for ever.
If we have forgotten the name of our God,
Or stretched out our hands to a strange god;
Shall not God search this out?
For he knoweth the secrets of the heart.
Yea, for thy sake are we killed all the day long;
We are counted as sheep for the slaughter.
Awake, why sleepest thou, O Lord?
Arise, cast us not off for ever.
Wherefore hidest thou thy face,
And forgettest our affliction and our oppression?
For our soul is bowed down to the dust:
Our belly cleaveth unto the earth.
Arise for our help,
And redeem us for thy mercies' sake.

Psalm XIV.

THE fool hath said in his heart, There is no God.
 { *They are corrupt, they have done abominable works,*
 { *There is none that doeth good.*
The LORD looked down from heaven upon the children of men,
 To see if there were any that did understand, and seek God.
They are all gone aside,
 { *They are all together become filthy:*
 { *There is none that doeth good, no, not one.*
Have all the workers of iniquity no knowledge?
 { *Who eat up my people as they eat bread,*
 { *And call not upon the* LORD.
There were they in great fear:
 For God is in the generation of the righteous.
Ye have shamed the counsel of the poor,
 Because the LORD *is his refuge.*
Oh that the salvation of Israel were come out of Zion!
 { *When the* LORD *bringeth back the captivity of his people,*
 { *Jacob shall rejoice, and Israel shall be glad.*

Psalm LXXXII.

GOD standeth in the congregation of the mighty;
 He judgeth among the gods.
How long will ye judge unjustly,
 And accept the persons of the wicked?
Defend the poor and fatherless:
 Do justice to the afflicted and needy.
Deliver the poor and needy:
 Rid them out of the hand of the wicked.
They know not, neither will they understand;
 { *They walk on in darkness:*
 { *All the foundations of the earth are out of course.*
I have said, Ye are gods;
 And all of you are children of the Most High.
But ye shall die like men,
 And fall like one of the princes.
Arise, O God, judge the earth:
 For thou shalt inherit all nations.

Lesson 44. (Page 95.)

Psalm XLIX.

HEAR this, all ye people;
 Give ear, all ye inhabitants of the world:
Both low and high,
 Rich and poor, together.
My mouth shall speak of wisdom;
 And the meditation of my heart shall be of understanding.
I will incline mine ear to a parable:
 I will open my dark saying upon the harp.
Wherefore should I fear in the days of evil,
 When the iniquity of my heels shall compass me about?
They that trust in their wealth,
 And boast themselves in the multitude of their riches;
None of them can by any means redeem his brother,
 Nor give to God a ransom for him:
For the redemption of their soul is precious,
 And it ceaseth for ever:
That he should still live for ever,
 And not see corruption.
For he seeth that wise men die,
 { *Likewise the fool and the brutish person perish,*
 { *And leave their wealth to others.*
Their inward thought is, that their houses shall continue for ever,
 { *And their dwelling places to all generations;*
 { *They call their lands after their own names.*
Nevertheless man being in honor abideth not:
 He is like the beasts that perish.
This their way is their folly:
 Yet their posterity approve their sayings.
Like sheep they are laid in the grave; death shall feed on them;
 { *The upright shall have dominion over them in the morning;*
 { *And their beauty shall consume in the grave from their dwelling.*
But God will redeem my soul from the power of the grave:
 For he shall receive me.
Be not thou afraid when one is made rich,
 When the glory of his house is increased;

For when he dieth he shall carry nothing away:
His glory shall not descend after him.
Though while he lived he blessed his soul:
And men will praise thee, when thou doest well to thyself:
He shall go to the generation of his fathers;
They shall never see light.
Man that is in honor, and understandeth not,
Is like the beasts that perish.

Psalm LVII.

BE merciful unto me, O God, be merciful unto me:
For my soul trusteth in thee:
   Yea, in the shadow of thy wings will I make my refuge,
   Until these calamities be overpast.
I will cry unto God most high;
Unto God that performeth all things for me.
He shall send from heaven, and save me
From the reproach of him that would swallow me up.
God shall send forth his mercy and his truth.
My soul is among lions:
And I lie even among them that are set on fire,
   Even the sons of men, whose teeth are spears and arrows,
   And their tongue a sharp sword.
Be thou exalted, O God, above the heavens;
Let thy glory be above all the earth.
They have prepared a net for my steps;
My soul is bowed down:
   They have digged a pit before me,
   Into the midst whereof they are fallen themselves.
My heart is fixed, O God, my heart is fixed:
I will sing and give praise.
Awake up, my glory;
Awake, psaltery and harp: I myself will awake early.
I will praise thee, O Lord, among the people:
I will sing unto thee among the nations.
For thy mercy is great unto the heavens,
And thy truth unto the clouds.
Be thou exalted, O God, above the heavens:
Let thy glory be above all the earth!

Lesson 45. (Page 97.)

PSALM L.

THE mighty God, even the LORD, hath spoken,
  { *And called the earth*
  { *From the rising of the sun unto the going down thereof.*
Out of Zion, the perfection of beauty,
  God hath shined.
Our God shall come, and shall not keep silence:
  { *A fire shall devour before him,*
  { *And it shall be very tempestuous round about him.*
He shall call to the heavens from above,
  And to the earth, that he may judge his people.
Gather my saints together unto me;
  Those that have made a covenant with me by sacrifice.
And the heavens shall declare his righteousness:
  For God is Judge himself.
Hear, O my people, and I will speak;
  { *O Israel, and I will testify against thee:*
  { *I am God, even thy God.*
I will not reprove thee for thy sacrifices,
  Or thy burnt offerings, to have been continually before me.
I will take no bullock out of thy house,
  Nor he-goats out of thy folds.
For every beast of the forest is mine,
  And the cattle upon a thousand hills.
I know all the fowls of the mountains:
  And the wild beasts of the field are mine.
If I were hungry, I would not tell thee:
  For the world is mine, and the fulness thereof.
Will I eat the flesh of bulls,
  Or drink the blood of goats?
Offer unto God thanksgiving;
  And pay thy vows unto the Most High:
And call upon me in the day of trouble:
  I will deliver thee, and thou shalt glorify me.
But unto the wicked God saith,
  { *What hast thou to do to declare my statutes,*
  { *Or that thou shouldest take my covenant in thy mouth?*

Seeing thou hatest instruction,
  And castest my words behind thee.
When thou sawest a thief, then thou consentedst with him,
  And hast been partaker with adulterers.
Thou givest thy mouth to evil,
  And thy tongue frameth deceit.
Thou sittest and speakest against thy brother;
  Thou slanderest thine own mother's son.
These things hast thou done, and I kept silence ;
  { Thou thoughtest that I was altogether such an one as thyself :
  { But I will reprove thee, and set them in order before thine eyes.
Now consider this, ye that forget God,
  Lest I tear you in pieces, and there be none to deliver.
Whoso offereth praise glorifieth me :
  { And to him that ordereth his conversation aright
  { Will I show the salvation of God.

Psalm XLVII.

OH clap your hands, all ye people ;
  Shout unto God with the voice of triumph.
For the LORD most high is terrible ;
  He is a great King over all the earth.
He shall subdue the people under us,
  And the nations under our feet.
He shall choose our inheritance for us,
  The excellency of Jacob whom he loved.
God is gone up with a shout,
  The LORD with the sound of a trumpet.
Sing praises to God, sing praises :
  Sing praises unto our King, sing praises.
For God is the King of all the earth :
  Sing ye praises with understanding.
God reigneth over the heathen :
  God sitteth upon the throne of his holiness.
The princes of the people are gathered together,
  Even the people of the God of Abraham :
For the shields of the earth belong unto God :
  He is greatly exalted.

Lesson 46. (Page 99.)

Psalm CI.

I WILL sing of mercy and judgment :
  Unto thee, O LORD, *will I sing.*
I will behave myself wisely in a perfect way.
  O when will thou come unto me?
  I will walk within my house with a perfect heart.
I will set no wicked thing before mine eyes :
  I hate the work of them that turn aside; it shall not cleave to me.
A froward heart shall depart from me :
  I will not know a wicked person.
Whoso privily slandereth his neighbor, him will I cut off :
  Him that hath an high look and a proud heart will I not suffer.
Mine eyes shall be upon the faithful of the land, that they may dwell with me :
  He that walketh in a perfect way, he shall serve me.
He that worketh deceit shall not dwell within my house :
  He that telleth lies shall not tarry in my sight.
I will early destroy all the wicked of the land ;
  That I may cut off all wicked doers from the city of the LORD.

Psalm LXXIII : 1—26.

TRULY God is good to Israel,
  Even to such as are of a clean heart.
But as for me, my feet were almost gone ;
  My steps had well nigh slipped.
For I was envious at the foolish,
  When I saw the prosperity of the wicked.
For there are no bands in their death :
  But their strength is firm.
They are not in trouble as other men ;
  Neither are they plagued like other men.
Therefore pride compasseth them about as a chain ;
  Violence covereth them as a garment.
Their eyes stand out with fatness :
  They have more than heart could wish.
They are corrupt, and speak wickedly concerning oppression :
  They speak loftily.

They set their mouth against the heavens,
And their tongue walketh through the earth.
Therefore his people return hither:
And waters of a full cup are wrung out to them.
And they say, How doth God know?
And is there knowledge in the Most High?
Behold, these are the ungodly, who prosper in the world;
They increase in riches.
Verily I have cleansed my heart in vain,
And washed my hands in innocency.
For all the day long have I been plagued,
And chastened every morning.
If I say, I will speak thus;
Behold, I should offend against the generation of thy children.
When I thought to know this,
It was too painful for me;
Until I went into the sanctuary of God;
Then understood I their end.
Surely thou didst set them in slippery places;
Thou castedst them down into destruction.
How are they brought into desolation, as in a moment!
They are utterly consumed with terrors.
As a dream when one awaketh;
So, O Lord, when thou awakest, thou shalt despise their image.
Thus my heart was grieved,
And I was pricked in my reins.
So foolish was I, and ignorant:
I was as a beast before thee.
Nevertheless I am continually with thee:
Thou hast holden me by my right hand.
Thou shalt guide me with thy counsel,
And afterward receive me to glory.
Whom have I in heaven but thee?
And there is none upon earth that I desire beside thee.
My flesh and my heart faileth:
But God is the strength of my heart, and my portion for ever.

Lesson 47. (Page 101.)

Psalm CXXIII.

UNTO thee lift I up mine eyes,
  O thou that dwellest in the heavens.
Behold, as the eyes of servants look unto the hand of their masters,
  And as the eyes of a maiden unto the hand of her mistress;
So our eyes wait upon the LORD our God,
  Until that he have mercy upon us.
Have mercy upon us, O LORD,
  Have mercy upon us: for we are exceedingly filled with contempt.
Our soul is exceedingly filled with the scorning of those that are at ease,
  And with the contempt of the proud.

Psalm CXXXIX.

O LORD, thou hast searched me, and known me.
  { Thou knowest my downsitting and mine uprising,
  { Thou understandest my thought afar off.
Thou compassest my path and my lying down,
  And art acquainted with all my ways.
For there is not a word in my tongue,
  But lo, O LORD, thou knowest it altogether.
Thou hast beset me behind and before,
  And laid thine hand upon me.
Such knowledge is too wonderful for me;
  It is high, I cannot attain unto it.
Whither shall I go from thy spirit?
  Or whither shall I flee from thy presence?
If I ascend up into heaven, thou art there:
  If I make my bed in hell, behold, thou art there.
If I take the wings of the morning,
  And dwell in the uttermost parts of the sea;
Even there shall thy hand lead me.
  And thy right hand shall hold me.
If I say, Surely the darkness shall cover me;
  Even the night shall be light about me.

Yea, the darkness hideth not from thee :
> But the night shineth as the day :
> The darkness and the light are both alike to thee.

For thou hast possessed my reins :
> Thou hast covered me in my mother's womb.

I will praise thee ; for I am fearfully and wonderfully made :
> Marvellous are thy works ; and that my soul knoweth right well.

My substance was not hid from thee, when I was made in secret,
> And curiously wrought in the lowest parts of the earth.

Thine eyes did see my substance, yet being unperfect ;
> And in thy book all my members were written,
> Which in continuance were fashioned, when as yet there was none of them.

How precious also are thy thoughts unto me, O God !
> How great is the sum of them !

If I should count them, they are more in number than the sand :
> When I awake, I am still with thee.

Surely thou wilt slay the wicked, O God !
> Depart from me, therefore, ye bloody men.

For they speak against thee wickedly,
> And thine enemies take thy name in vain.

Do not I hate them, O LORD, that hate thee ?
> And am I not grieved with those that rise up against thee?

I hate them with perfect hatred :
> I count them mine enemies.

Search me, O God, and know my heart :
> Try me, and know my thoughts :

And see if there be any wicked way in me,
> And lead me in the way everlasting.

Lesson 48. (Page 102.)

From Psalm LXXVIII.

GIVE ear, O my people, to my law :
> Incline your ears to the words of my mouth.

I will open my mouth in a parable :
> I will utter dark sayings of old :

Which we have heard and known,
> And our fathers have told us.

We will not hide them from their children,
> Showing to the generation to come the praises of the LORD,
> And his strength, and his wonderful works that he hath done.
> For he established a testimony in Jacob,
> And appointed a law in Israel,
>> Which he commanded our fathers,
>> That they should make them known to their children:
That the generation to come might know them,
>> Even the children which should be born;
>> Who should arise and declare them to their children:
That they might set their hope in God,
> And not forget the works of God, but keep his commandments:
> And might not be as their fathers,
> A stubborn and rebellious generation;
>> A generation that set not their heart aright,
>> And whose spirit was not steadfast with God.
> The children of Ephraim, being armed, and carrying bows,
> Turned back in the day of battle.
> They kept not the covenant of God, and refused to walk in his law.
And forgat his works,
> And his wonders that he had showed them.
Marvellous things did he in the sight of their fathers,
> In the land of Egypt, in the field of Zoan.
He divided the sea, and caused them to pass through;
> And he made the waters to stand as an heap.
In the daytime also he led them with a cloud,
> And all the night with a light of fire.
He clave the rocks in the wilderness,
> And gave them drink as out of the great depths.
He brought streams also out of the rock,
> And caused waters to run down like rivers.
> And they sinned yet more against him
> By provoking the Most High in the wilderness.
> And they tempted God in their heart by asking meat for their lust.
Yea, they spake against God:
> They said, Can God furnish a table in the wilderness?
> Behold, he smote the rock, that the waters gushed out,
> And the streams overflowed;
> Can he give bread also? Can he provide flesh for his people?
Therefore the LORD heard this, and was wroth;
> So a fire was kindled against Jacob,
> And anger also came up against Israel;

Because they believed not in God,
And trusted not in his salvation:
Though he had commanded the clouds from above,
And opened the doors of heaven.
And had rained down manna upon them to eat,
And had given them of the corn of heaven.
Man did eat angels' food:
He sent them meat to the full.
For all this they sinned still,
And believed not for his wondrous works.
Therefore their days did he consume in vanity,
And their years in trouble.
When he slew them, then they sought him:
And they returned and inquired early after God.
And they remembered that God was their rock,
And the high God their redeemer.
Nevertheless they did flatter him with their mouth,
And they lied unto him with their tongues.
For their heart was not right with him,
Neither were they steadfast in his covenant.
{ But he, being full of compassion, forgave their iniquity,
{ And destroyed them not:
　{ *Yea, many a time turned he his anger away,*
　{ *And did not stir up all his wrath.*
For he remembered that they were but flesh:
A wind that passeth away, and cometh not again.
He cast out the heathen also before them,
　{ *And divided them an inheritance by line,*
　{ *And made the tribes of Israel to dwell in their tents.*
Yet they tempted and provoked the most high God,
And kept not his testimonies:
But turned back, and dealt unfaithfully like their fathers:
They were turned aside like a deceitful bow.
For they provoked him to anger with their high places,
And moved him to jealousy with their graven images.
Moreover he refused the tabernacle of Joseph,
And chose not the tribe of Ephraim:
But chose the tribe of Judah,
The mount Zion which he loved.
And he built his sanctuary like high palaces,
Like the earth which he hath established for ever.
He chose David also his servant,
And took him from the sheepfolds:

From following the ewes great with young
{ He brought him to feed Jacob his people,
{ And Israel his inheritance.
So he fed them according to the integrity of his heart;
And guided them by the skillfulness of his hands.

Lesson 49. (Page 105.)

Psalm XXXIX.

I SAID, I will take heed to my ways, that I sin not with my tongue:
I will keep my mouth with a bridle, while the wicked is before me.
I was dumb with silence,
I held my peace, even from good; and my sorrow was stirred.
My heart was hot within me,
While I was musing the fire burned:
Then spake I with my tongue, LORD, make me to know mine end,
{ And the measure of my days, what it is;
{ That I may know how frail I am.
Behold, thou hast made my days as an handbreadth;
{ And mine age is as nothing before thee:
{ Verily every man at his best state is altogether vanity.
Surely every man walketh in a vain show:
{ Surely they are disquieted in vain:
{ He heapeth up riches, and knoweth not who shall gather them.
And now, Lord, what wait I for?
My hope is in thee.
Deliver me from all my transgressions:
Make me not the reproach of the foolish.
I was dumb, I opened not my mouth;
Because thou didst it.
Remove thy stroke away from me:
I am consumed by the blow of thine hand.
When thou with rebukes dost correct man for iniquity,
{ Thou makest his beauty to consume away like a moth:
{ Surely every man is vanity.
Hear my prayer, O LORD, and give ear unto my cry;
Hold not thy peace at my tears.

> For I am a stranger with thee,
> *And a sojourner, as all my fathers were.*
> O spare me, that I may recover strength,
> *Before I go hence, and be no more.*

Psalm LXXI.

> IN thee, O LORD, do I put my trust:
> *Let me never be put to confusion.*
> Deliver me in thy righteousness, and cause me to escape:
> *Incline thine ear unto me, and save me.*
> Be thou my strong habitation, whereunto I may continually resort:
> *Thou hast given commandment to save me;*
> *For thou art my rock and my fortress.*
> Deliver me, O my God, out of the hand of the wicked.
> *Out of the hand of the unrighteous and cruel man.*
> For thou art my hope, O Lord GOD:
> *Thou art my trust from my youth.*
> By thee have I been holden up from the womb:
> *Thou art he that took me out of my mother's womb:*
> *My praise shall be continually of thee.*
> I am as a wonder unto many;
> *But thou art my strong refuge.*
> Let my mouth be filled with thy praise
> *And with thy honor all the day.*
> Cast me not off in the time of old age;
> *Forsake me not when my strength faileth.*
> For mine enemies speak against me;
> *And they that lay wait for my soul take counsel together,*
> Saying, God hath forsaken him:
> *Persecute and take him; for there is none to deliver him.*
> O God, be not far from me:
> *O my God, make haste for my help.*
> Let them be confounded and consumed that are adversaries to my soul;
> *Let them be covered with reproach and dishonor that seek my hurt.*
> But I will hope continually,
> *And will yet praise thee more and more.*
> My mouth shall show forth thy righteousness,
> *And thy salvation all the day: for I know not the numbers thereof.*
> I will go in the strength of the Lord GOD:
> *I will make mention of thy righteousness, even of thine only.*
> O God, thou hast taught me from my youth:
> *And hitherto have I declared thy wondrous works.*

Now also when I am old and grayheaded, O God, forsake me not;
   Until I have showed thy strength unto this generation.
   And thy power to every one that is to come.
Thy righteousness also, O God, is very high,
   Who hast done great things: O God, who is like unto thee!
Thou, which hast showed me great and sore troubles, shalt quicken me again,
   And shalt bring me up again from the depths of the earth;
Thou shalt increase my greatness,
   And comfort me on every side.
I will also praise thee with the psaltery, even thy truth, O my God;
   Unto thee will I sing with the harp, O thou Holy One of Israel.
My lips shall greatly rejoice when I sing unto thee;
   And my soul, which thou hast redeemed.
My tongue also shall talk of thy righteousness all the day long:
   For they are confounded, for they are brought unto shame, that seek my hurt.

Lesson 50. (Page 107.)

Psalm CXIX : 97—128.

OH how love I thy law!
   It is my meditation all the day.
Thou, through thy commandments, hast made me wiser than mine enemies:
   For they are ever with me.
I have more understanding than all my teachers:
   For thy testimonies are my meditation.
I understand more than the ancients,
   Because I keep thy precepts.
I have refrained my feet from every evil way,
   That I might keep thy word.
I have not departed from thy judgments:
   For thou hast taught me.
How sweet are thy words unto my taste!
   Yea, sweeter than honey to my mouth.
Through thy precepts I get understanding:
   Therefore I hate every false way.
Thy word is a lamp unto my feet,
   And a light unto my path.

I have sworn, and I will perform it,
   That I will keep thy righteous judgments.
I am afflicted very much:
   Quicken me, O Lord, according unto thy word.
Accept, I beseech thee, the freewill offerings of my mouth, O Lord,
   And teach me thy judgments.
My soul is continually in my hand:
   Yet do I not forget thy law.
The wicked have laid a snare for me:
   Yet I erred not from thy precepts.
Thy testimonies have I taken as a heritage for ever:
   For they are the rejoicing of my heart.
I have inclined mine heart to perform thy statutes
   Alway, even unto the end.
I hate vain thoughts:
   But thy law do I love.
Thou art my hiding-place and my shield:
   I hope in thy word.
Depart from me, ye evil doers:
   For I will keep the commandments of my God.
Uphold me according unto thy word, that I may live:
   And let me not be ashamed of my hope.
Hold thou me up, and I shall be safe:
   And I will have respect unto thy statutes continually.
Thou hast trodden down all them that err from thy statutes:
   For their deceit is falsehood.
Thou puttest away all the wicked of the earth like dross:
   Therefore I love thy testimonies.
My flesh trembleth for fear of thee;
   And I am afraid of thy judgments.
I have done judgment and justice:
   Leave me not to mine oppressors.
Be surety for thy servant for good:
   Let not the proud oppress me.
Mine eyes fail for thy salvation,
   And for the word of thy righteousness.
Deal with thy servant according unto thy mercy,
   And teach me thy statutes.
I am thy servant; give me understanding,
   That I may know thy testimonies.
It is time for thee, Lord, to work:
   For they have made void thy law.

Therefore I love thy commandments
Above gold; yea, above fine gold.
Therefore I esteem all thy precepts concerning all things to be right;
And I hate every false way.

Lesson 51. (Page 109.)

Psalm CXIX : 129—160.

THY testimonies are wonderful:
Therefore doth my soul keep them.
The entrance of thy words giveth light;
It giveth understanding unto the simple.
I opened my mouth, and panted :
For I longed for thy commandments.
Look thou upon me, and be merciful unto me,
As thou usest to do unto those that love thy name.
Order my steps in thy word :
And let not any iniquity have dominion over me.
Deliver me from the oppression of man :
So will I keep thy precepts.
Make thy face to shine upon thy servant;
And teach me thy statutes.
Rivers of water run down mine eyes,
Because they keep not thy law.
Righteous art thou, O Lord,
And upright are thy judgments.
Thy testimonies that thou hast commanded are righteous
And very faithful.
My zeal hath consumed me,
Because mine enemies have forgotten thy words.
Thy word is very pure:
Therefore thy servant loveth it.
I am small and despised :
Yet do not I forget thy precepts.
Thy righteousness is an everlasting righteousness,
And thy law is the truth.
Trouble and anguish have taken hold on me :
Yet thy commandments are my delights.

The righteousness of thy testimonies is everlasting:
   Give me understanding, and I shall live.
I cried with my whole heart; hear me, O LORD:
   I will keep thy statutes.
I cried unto thee;
   Save me, and I shall keep thy testimonies.
I prevented the dawning of the morning, and cried:
   I hoped in thy word.
Mine eyes prevent the night watches,
   That I might meditate in thy word.
Hear my voice, according unto thy loving-kindness:
   O LORD, quicken me according to thy judgment.
They draw nigh that follow after mischief:
   They are far from thy law.
Thou art near, O LORD;
   And all thy commandments are truth.
Concerning thy testimonies, I have known of old
   That thou hast founded them for ever.
Consider mine affliction, and deliver me:
   For I do not forget thy law.
Plead my cause, and deliver me:
   Quicken me according to thy word.
Salvation is far from the wicked:
   For they seek not thy statutes.
Great are thy tender mercies, O LORD:
   Quicken me according to thy judgments.
Many are my persecutors and mine enemies;
   Yet do I not decline from thy testimonies.
I beheld the transgressors, and was grieved;
   Because they kept not thy word.
Consider how I love thy precepts:
   Quicken me, O LORD, according to thy loving-kindness.
Thy word is true from the beginning:
   And every one of thy righteous judgments endureth for ever.

Lesson 52. (Page 111.)

Psalm LV.

GIVE ear to my prayer, O God;
And hide not thyself from my supplication.
Attend unto me and hear me;
I mourn in my complaint, and make a noise;
Because of the voice of the enemy, because of the oppression of the wicked:
For they cast iniquity upon me, and in wrath they hate me.
My heart is sore pained within me:
And the terrors of death are fallen upon me.
Fearfulness and trembling are come upon me,
And horror hath overwhelmed me.
And I said, Oh that I had wings like a dove!
For then would I fly away, and be at rest.
Lo, then would I wander far off,
And remain in the wilderness.
I would hasten my escape,
From the windy storm and tempest.
Destroy, O LORD, and divide their tongues:
For I have seen violence and strife in the city.
Day and night they go about it upon the walls thereof:
Mischief, also, and sorrow, are in the midst of it.
Wickedness is in the midst thereof:
Deceit and guile depart not from her streets.
For it was not an enemy that reproached me: then could I have borne it;
{ *Neither was it he that hated me that did magnify himself against me;*
{ *Then I would have hid myself from him:*
But it was thou, a man mine equal, my guide, and mine acquaintance.
{ *We took sweet counsel together,*
{ *And walked unto the house of God in company.*
Let death seize upon them, and let them go down quick into hell:
For wickedness is in their dwellings, and among them.
As for me, I will call upon God;
And the LORD shall save me.
Evening, and morning, and at noon, will I pray, and cry aloud:
And he shall hear my voice.
He hath delivered my soul in peace from the battle that was against me:
For there were many with me.

God shall hear, and afflict them, even he that abideth of old.
    Because they have no changes, therefore they fear not God.
He hath put forth his hands against such as be at peace with him:
    He hath broken his covenant.
The words of his mouth were smoother than butter, but war was in his heart:
    His words were softer than oil, yet were they drawn swords.
Cast thy burden upon the LORD, and he shall sustain thee:
    He shall never suffer the righteous to be moved.
But thou, O God, shalt bring them down into the pit of destruction:
    { *Bloody and deceitful men shall not live out half their days;*
    { *But I will trust in thee.*

Psalm LVI.

BE merciful unto me, O God: for man would swallow me up;
    He fighting daily oppresseth me.
Mine enemies would daily swallow me up:
    For they be many that fight against me, O thou Most High.
What time I am afraid, I will trust in thee.
    In God I will praise his word,
In God I have put my trust;
    I will not fear what flesh can do unto me.
Every day they wrest my words:
    All their thoughts are against me for evil.
They gather themselves together,
    They hide themselves, they mark my steps, when they wait for my soul.
Shall they escape by iniquity?
    In thine anger cast down the people, O God.
Thou tellest my wanderings:
    Put thou my tears into thy bottle: are they not in thy book?
When I cry unto thee, then shall mine enemies turn back:
    This I know; for God is for me.
In God will I praise his word:
    In the LORD will I praise his word.
In God have I put my trust:
    I will not be afraid what man can do unto me.
Thy vows are upon me, O God:
    I will render praises unto thee.
For thou hast delivered my soul from death:
    { *Wilt not thou deliver my feet from falling,*
    { *That I may walk before God in the light of the living?*

Lesson 53. (Page 113.)

Psalm CII.

HEAR my prayer, O Lord,
 And let my cry come unto thee.
Hide not thy face from me in the day when I am in trouble;
 { Incline thine ear unto me:
 { In the day when I call answer me speedily.
For my days are consumed like smoke,
 And my bones are burned as a hearth.
My heart is smitten, and withered like grass ;
 So that I forget to eat my bread.
By reason of the voice of my groaning my bones cleave to my skin.
 I am like a pelican of the wilderness : I am like an owl of the desert.
I watch, and am as a sparrow alone upon the housetop.
 { Mine enemies reproach me all the day ;
 { And they that are mad against me are sworn against me.
For I have eaten ashes like bread,
 And mingled my drink with weeping.
Because of thine indignation and thy wrath:
 For thou hast lifted me up, and cast me down.
My days are like a shadow that declineth ;
 And I am withered like grass.
But thou, O Lord, shalt endure for ever ;
 And thy remembrance unto all generations.
Thou shalt arise, and have mercy upon Zion :
 For the time to favor her, yea, the set time, is come.
For thy servants take pleasure in her stones,
 And favor the dust thereof.
So the heathen shall fear the name of the Lord,
 And all the kings of the earth thy glory.
When the Lord shall build up Zion,
 He shall appear in his glory.
He will regard the prayer of the destitute,
 And not despise their prayer.
This shall be written for the generation to come,
 And the people which shall be created shall praise the Lord.
For he hath looked down from the height of his sanctuary ;
 From heaven did the Lord behold the earth ;

To hear the groaning of the prisoner ;
  To loose those that are appointed to death ;
To declare the name of the LORD in Zion,
  And his praise in Jerusalem ;
When the people are gathered together,
  And the kingdoms, to serve the LORD.
He weakened my strength in the way ;
  He shortened my days.
I said, O my God, take me not away in the midst of my days :
  Thy years are throughout all generations.
Of old hast thou laid the foundation of the earth :
  And the heavens are the work of thy hands.
They shall perish, but thou shalt endure :
  Yea, all of them shall wax old like a garment ;
As a vesture shalt thou change them, and they shall be changed :
  But thou art the same, and thy years shall have no end.
The children of thy servants shall continue,
  And their seed shall be established before thee.

PSALM XIII.

HOW long wilt thou forget me, O LORD ?
  For ever ? how long wilt thou hide thy face from me?
{ How long shall I take counsel in my soul,
  Having sorrow in my heart daily ?
  How long shall mine enemy be exalted over me?
Consider and hear me, O LORD my God :
  Lighten mine eyes, lest I sleep the sleep of death :
Lest mine enemy say, I have prevailed against him ;
  And those that trouble me rejoice when I am moved.
But I have trusted in thy mercy ;
  My heart shall rejoice in thy salvation.
I will sing unto the LORD,
  Because he hath dealt bountifully with me.

Lesson 54. (Page 115.)

Psalm CXLIII.

HEAR my prayer, O Lord,
  Give ear to my supplications:
  In thy faithfulness answer me, and in thy righteousness.
And enter not into judgment with thy servant:
  For in thy sight shall no man living be justified.
For the enemy hath persecuted my soul;
He hath smitten my life down to the ground;
  He hath made me to dwell in darkness, as those that have been long dead.
Therefore is my spirit overwhelmed within me;
  My heart within me is desolate.
I remember the days of old:
  I meditate on all thy works; I muse on the work of thy hands.
I stretch forth my hands unto thee:
  My soul thirsteth after thee, as a thirsty land.
Hear me speedily, O Lord: my spirit faileth:
  Hide not thy face from me,
  Lest I be like unto them that go down into the pit.
Cause me to hear thy loving-kindness in the morning;
For in thee do I trust:
  Cause me to know the way wherein I should walk;
  For I lift up my soul unto thee.
Deliver me, O Lord, from mine enemies:
  I flee unto thee to hide me.
Teach me to do thy will; for thou art my God:
  Thy spirit is good; lead me into the land of uprightness.
Quicken me, O Lord, for thy name's sake:
  For thy righteousness' sake bring my soul out of trouble.
And of thy mercy cut off mine enemies,
  And destroy all them that afflict my soul: for I am thy servant.

Psalm XL.

I WAITED patiently for the Lord;
  And he inclined unto me, and heard my cry.
He brought me up also out of an horrible pit, out of the miry clay,
  And set my feet upon a rock, and established my goings.

And he hath put a new song in my mouth, even praise unto our God:
Many shall see it, and fear, and shall trust in the LORD.
Blessed is that man that maketh the LORD his trust,
And respecteth not the proud, nor such as turn aside to lies.
Many, O LORD my God, are thy wonderful works which thou hast done,
And thy thoughts which are to us-ward:
They cannot be reckoned up in order unto thee:
If I would declare and speak of them, they are more than can be numbered.
Sacrifice and offering thou didst not desire:
{ *Mine ears hast thou opened:*
{ *Burnt offering and sin offering hast thou not required.*
Then said I, Lo, I come:
In the volume of the book it is written of me,
I delight to do thy will, O my God:
Yea, thy law is within my heart.
I have preached righteousness in the great congregation:
Lo, I have not refrained my lips, O LORD, thou knowest.
I have not hid thy righteousness within my heart;
{ *I have declared thy faithfulness and thy salvation:*
{ *I have not concealed thy loving-kindness and thy truth from the great con-*
{ *gregation.*
Withhold not thou thy tender mercies from me, O LORD:
Let thy loving-kindness and thy truth continually preserve me.
For innumerable evils have compassed me about:
{ *Mine iniquities have taken hold upon me,*
{ *So that I am not able to look up;*
They are more than the hairs of mine head:
Therefore my heart faileth me.
Be pleased, O LORD, to deliver me:
O LORD, make haste to help me.
{ Let them be ashamed and confounded together
{ That seek after my soul to destroy it;
Let them be driven backward and put to shame that wish me evil.
Let them be desolate for a reward of their shame
That say unto me, Aha! aha!
Let all those that seek thee rejoice and be glad in thee:
Let such as love thy salvation say continually, The LORD be magnified.
But I am poor and needy; yet the Lord thinketh upon me:
Thou art my help and my deliverer; make no tarrying, O my God.

Lesson 55. (Page 117.)

Psalm LXXXVIII.

O LORD God of my salvation,
    I have cried day and night before thee:
Let my prayer come before thee:
    Incline thine ear unto my cry;
For my soul is full of troubles:
    And my life draweth nigh unto the grave.
I am counted with them that go down into the pit:
    I am as a man that hath no strength:
Free among the dead, like the slain that lie in the grave,
    Whom thou rememberest no more: and they are cut off from thy hand.
Thou hast laid me in the lowest pit,
    In darkness, in the deeps.
Thy wrath lieth hard upon me,
    And thou hast afflicted me with all thy waves.
Thou hast put away mine acquaintance far from me;
    { *Thou hast made me an abomination unto them:*
    { *I am shut up, and I cannot come forth.*
Mine eye mourneth by reason of affliction:
    LORD, *I have called daily upon thee, I have stretched out my hands unto thee.*
Wilt thou show wonders to the dead?
    Shall the dead arise, and praise thee?
Shall thy loving-kindness be declared in the grave?
    Or thy faithfulness in destruction?
Shall thy wonders be known in the dark?
    And thy righteousness in the land of forgetfulness?
But unto thee have I cried, O LORD:
    And in the morning shall my prayer prevent thee.
LORD, why castest thou off my soul?
    Why hidest thou thy face from me?
I am afflicted and ready to die from my youth up:
    While I suffer thy terrors I am distracted.
Thy fierce wrath goeth over me;
    Thy terrors have cut me off.
They came round about me daily like water;
    They compassed me about together.
Lover and friend hast thou put far from me,
    And mine acquaintance into darkness.

Psalm LXIX.

SAVE me, O God;
  For the waters are come in unto my soul.
I sink in deep mire, where there is no standing:
  I am come into deep waters, where the floods overflow me.
I am weary of my crying: my throat is dried:
  Mine eyes fail while I wait for my God.
They that hate me without a cause are more than the hairs of mine head:
  { *They that would destroy me, being mine enemies wrongfully, are mighty:*
  { *Then I restored that which I took not away.*
O God, thou knowest my foolishness;
  And my sins are not hid from thee.
{ Let not them that wait on thee, O Lord GOD of hosts,
{ Be ashamed for my sake:
  { *Let not those that seek thee be confounded for my sake,*
  { *O God of Israel.*
Because for thy sake I have borne reproach:
  Shame hath covered my face.
I am become a stranger unto my brethren,
  And an alien unto my mother's children.
For the zeal of thine house hath eaten me up;
  And the reproaches of them that reproached thee are fallen upon me.
When I wept, and chastened my soul with fasting,
  That was to my reproach.
I made sackcloth also my garment;
  And I became a proverb to them.
They that sit in the gate speak against me;
  And I was the song of the drunkards.
But as for me, my prayer is unto thee, O LORD, in an acceptable time:
  O God, in the multitude of thy mercy hear me, in the truth of thy salvatio
Deliver me out of the mire, and let me not sink:
  Let me be delivered from them that hate me, and out of the deep waters.
Let not the waterflood overflow me,
  { *Neither let the deep swallow me up,*
  { *And let not the pit shut her mouth upon me.*
Hear me, O LORD; for thy loving-kindness is good:
  Turn unto me according to the multitude of thy tender mercies.
And hide not thy face from thy servant;
  For I am in trouble: hear me speedily.
Draw nigh unto my soul, and redeem it:
  Deliver me because of mine enemies.

Thou hast known my reproach, and my shame, and my dishonor:
Mine adversaries are all before thee.
Reproach hath broken my heart; and I am full of heaviness:
{ *And I looked for some to take pity, but there was none ;*
{ *And for comforters, but I found none.*
They gave me also gall for my meat ;
And in my thirst they gave me vinegar to drink.
Let their table become a snare before them :
And that which should have been for their welfare, let it become a trap.
Let their eyes be darkened, that they see not ;
And make their loins continually to shake.
Pour out thine indignation upon them,
And let thy wrathful anger take hold of them.
Let their habitation be desolate ;
And let none dwell in their tents,
For they persecute him whom thou hast smitten ;
And they talk to the grief of those whom thou hast wounded.
Add iniquity unto their iniquity :
And let them not come into thy righteousness.
Let them be blotted out of the book of the living,
And not be written with the righteous.
But I am poor and sorrowful :
Let thy salvation, O God, set me up on high.
I will praise the name of God with a song,
And will magnify him with thanksgiving.
This also shall please the LORD,
Better than an ox or bullock that hath horns and hoofs.
The humble shall see this, and be glad :
And your heart shall live that seek God.
For the LORD heareth the poor,
And despiseth not his prisoners.
Let the heaven and earth praise him,
The seas, and every thing that moveth therein.
For God will save Zion, and will build the cities of Judah :
That they may dwell there, and have it in possession.
The seed also of his servants shall inherit it :
And they that love his name shall dwell therein.

Lesson 56. (Page 120.)

Psalm X.

WHY standest thou afar off, O Lord?
Why hidest thou thyself in times of trouble?
The wicked in his pride doth persecute the poor:
Let them be taken in the devices that they have imagined.
For the wicked boasteth of his heart's desire,
And blesseth the covetous, whom the Lord abhorreth.
The wicked, through the pride of his countenance, will not seek after God:
God is not in all his thoughts.
His ways are always grievous;
{ *Thy judgments are far above out of his sight:*
{ *As for all his enemies, he puffeth at them.*
He hath said in his heart, I shall not be moved:
For I shall never be in adversity.
His mouth is full of cursing and deceit and fraud:
Under his tongue is mischief and vanity.
He sitteth in the lurking places of the villages:
{ *In the secret places doth he murder the innocent:*
{ *His eyes are privily set against the poor.*
He lieth in wait secretly, as a lion in his den:
{ *He lieth in wait to catch the poor:*
{ *He doth catch the poor, when he draweth him into his net.*
He croucheth, and humbleth himself,
That the poor may fall by his strong ones.
He hath said in his heart, God hath forgotten:
He hideth his face; he will never see it.
Arise, O Lord; O God, lift up thine hand:
Forget not the humble.
Wherefore doth the wicked contemn God?
He hath said in his heart, Thou wilt not require it.
{ Thou hast seen it:
{ For thou beholdest mischief and spite, to requite it with thy hand:
The poor committeth himself unto thee; thou art the helper of the fatherless.
Break thou the arm of the wicked and the evil man:
Seek out his wickedness till thou find none.
The Lord is King for ever and ever:
The heathen are perished out of his land.

LORD, thou hast heard the desire of the humble:
   Thou wilt prepare their heart, thou wilt cause thine ear to hear:
To judge the fatherless and the oppressed,
   That the man of the earth may no more oppress.

PSALM LIX.

DELIVER me from mine enemies, O my God:
   Defend me from them that rise up against me.
Deliver me from the workers of iniquity,
   And save me from bloody men.
For, lo, they lie in wait for my soul:
   { *The mighty are gathered against me;*
   { *Not for my transgression, nor for my sin, O* LORD.
They run, and prepare themselves without my fault:
   Awake to help me, and behold.
{ Thou therefore, O LORD God of hosts, the God of Israel,
{ Awake to visit all the heathen:
   Be not merciful to any wicked transgressors.
They return at evening:
   They make a noise like a dog, and go round about the city.
Behold, they belch out with their mouth:
   Swords are in their lips: for who, say they, doth hear?
But thou, O LORD, shalt laugh at them;
   Thou shalt have all the heathen in derision.
Because of his strength will I wait upon thee:
   For God is my defence.
The God of my mercy shall prevent me:
   God shall let me see my desire upon mine enemies.
Slay them not, lest my people forget:
   { *Scatter them by thy power;*
   { *And bring them down, O Lord our shield.*
{ For the sin of their mouth and the words of their lips
{ Let them even be taken in their pride:
   And for cursing and lying which they speak.
Consume them in wrath, consume them, that they may not be:
   { *And let them know that God ruleth in Jacob,*
   { *Unto the ends of the earth.*
And at evening let them return;
   And let them make a noise like a dog, and go round about the city.
Let them wander up and down for meat,
   And grudge if they be not satisfied.

But I will sing of thy power;
- Yea, I will sing aloud of thy mercy in the morning:
- For thou hast been my defence and refuge in the day of my trouble.

Unto thee, O my strength, will I sing:
For God is my defence, and the God of my mercy.

Lesson 57. (Page 122.)

Psalm XII.

HELP, Lord; for the godly man ceaseth;
For the faithful fail from among the children of men.
They speak vanity every one with his neighbor:
With flattering lips, and with a double heart, do they speak.
The Lord shall cut off all flattering lips,
And the tongue that speaketh proud things:
Who have said, With our tongue will we prevail;
Our lips are our own: who is lord over us?
- For the oppression of the poor, for the sighing of the needy,
- Now will I arise, saith the Lord;

I will set him in safety, from him that puffeth at him.
The words of the Lord are pure words:
As silver tried in a furnace of earth, purified seven times.
Thou shalt keep them, O Lord,
Thou shalt preserve them from this generation, for ever.
The wicked walk on every side,
When the vilest men are exalted.

Psalm LIII.

THE fool hath said in his heart, There is no God.
- Corrupt are they, and have done abominable iniquity:
- There is none that doeth good.

God looked down from heaven upon the children of men,
- To see if there were any that did understand,
- That did seek God.

Every one of them is gone back:
- They are altogether become filthy;
- There is none that doeth good, no, not one.

Have the workers of iniquity no knowledge?
{ Who eat up my people as they eat bread:
{ They have not called upon God.
There were they in great fear, where no fear was:
{ For God hath scattered the bones of him that encampeth against thee:
{ Thou hast put them to shame, because God hath despised them.
Oh that the salvation of Israel were come out of Zion!
{ When God bringeth back the captivity of his people,
{ Jacob shall rejoice, and Israel shall be glad.

PSALM LX.

O GOD, thou hast cast us off, thou hast scattered us,
Thou hast been displeased; O turn thyself to us again.
Thou hast made the earth to tremble; thou hast broken it:
Heal the breaches thereof; for it shaketh.
Thou hast showed thy people hard things:
Thou hast made us to drink the wine of astonishment.
Thou hast given a banner to them that feared thee,
That it may be displayed because of the truth.
That thy beloved may be delivered;
Save with thy right hand, and hear me.
God hath spoken in his holiness;
{ I will rejoice, I will divide Shechem,
{ And mete out the valley of Succoth.
Gilead is mine, and Manasseh is mine;
{ Ephraim also is the strength of mine head;
{ Judah is my lawgiver;
Moab is my washpot; over Edom will I cast out my shoe:
Philistia, triumph thou because of me.
Who will bring me into the strong city?
Who will lead me into Edom?
Wilt not thou, O God, which hadst cast us off?
And thou, O God, which didst not go out with our armies?
Give us help from trouble:
For vain is the help of man.
Through God we shall do valiantly:
For he it is that shall tread down our enemies.

Lesson 58. (Page 124.)

From Psalm XXII.

MY God, my God, why hast thou forsaken me?
  Why art thou so far from helping me, and from the words of my roaring?
O my God, I cry in the daytime, but thou hearest not;
  And in the night season, and am not silent.
But thou art holy,
  O thou that inhabitest the praises of Israel.
Our fathers trusted in thee:
  They trusted, and thou didst deliver them.
They cried unto thee, and were delivered:
  They trusted in thee, and were not confounded.
But I am a worm, and no man;
  A reproach of men, and despised of the people.
All they that see me laugh me to scorn:
  They shoot out the lip, they shake the head,
Saying, He trusted on the LORD that he would deliver him:
  Let him deliver him, seeing he delighted in him.
But thou art he that took me out of the womb:
  Thou didst make me hope when I was upon my mother's breasts.
My strength is dried up like a potsherd;
  { *And my tongue cleaveth to my jaws;*
  { *And thou hast brought me into the dust of death.*
For dogs have compassed me:
  { *The assembly of the wicked have inclosed me:*
  { *They pierced my hands and my feet.*
I may tell all my bones:
  They look and stare upon me.
They part my garments among them,
  And cast lots upon my vesture.
But be not thou far from me, O LORD:
  O my strength, haste thee to help me!
I will declare thy name unto my brethren:
  In the midst of the congregation will I praise thee.
Ye that fear the LORD, praise him;
  All ye the seed of Jacob, glorify him; and fear him, all ye the seed of Israel.
For he hath not despised nor abhorred the affliction of the afflicted:
  Neither hath he hid his face from him; but when he cried unto him, he heard.

My praise shall be of thee in the great congregation:
>   *I will pay my vows before them that fear him.*

The meek shall eat and be satisfied:
>   *They shall praise the* LORD *that seek him: your heart shall live for ever.*

All the ends of the world shall remember and turn unto the LORD:
>   *And all the kindreds of the nations shall worship before thee.*

For the kingdom is the LORD's:
>   *And he is governor among the nations.*

FROM PSALM XXXI.

IN thee, O LORD, do I put my trust;
>   *Let me never be ashamed: deliver me in thy righteousness.*

Bow down thine ear to me; deliver me speedily:
>   *Be thou my strong rock, for an house of defence to save me.*

For thou art my rock and my fortress;
>   *Therefore for thy name's sake lead me, and guide me.*

Pull me out of the net that they have laid privily for me:
>   *For thou art my strength.*

Into thine hand I commit my spirit:
>   *Thou hast redeemed me, O* LORD *God of truth.*

I have hated them that regard lying vanities:
>   *But I trust in the* LORD.

Oh how great is thy goodness, which thou hast laid up for them that fear thee;
>   *Which thou hast wrought for them that trust in thee before the sons of men.*

Thou shalt hide them in the secret of thy presence from the pride of man:
>   *Thou shalt keep them secretly in a pavilion from the strife of tongues.*

Blessed be the LORD:
>   *For he hath showed me his marvellous kindness in a strong city.*

For I said in my haste, I am cut off from before thine eyes:
>   *{ Nevertheless thou heardest the voice of my supplications,*
>   *{ When I cried unto thee.*

O love the LORD, all ye his saints:
>   *{ For the* LORD *preserveth the faithful,*
>   *{ And plentifully rewardeth the proud doer.*

Be of good courage, and he shall strengthen your heart,
>   *All ye that hope in the* LORD.

Lesson 59. (Page 126.)

From Psalm LXIX.

SAVE me, O God;
   For the waters are come in unto my soul.
I sink in deep mire, where there is no standing:
   I am come into deep waters, where the floods overflow me.
I am weary of my crying: my throat is dried:
   Mine eyes fail while I wait for my God.
{ Let not them that wait on thee, O Lord God of hosts,
{ Be ashamed for my sake:
   { *Let not those that seek thee be confounded for my sake,*
   { *O God of Israel.*
Because for thy sake I have borne reproach:
   Shame hath covered my face.
I am become a stranger unto my brethren,
   And an alien unto my mother's children.
For the zeal of thine house hath eaten me up;
   And the reproaches of them that reproached thee are fallen upon me.
But as for me, my prayer is unto thee, O Lord, in an acceptable time:
   O God, in the multitude of thy mercy hear me, in the truth of thy salvation.
Deliver me out of the mire, and let me not sink:
   Let me be delivered from them that hate me, and out of the deep waters.
Let not the waterflood overflow me,
   { *Neither let the deep swallow me up,*
   { *And let not the pit shut her mouth upon me.*
Hear me, O Lord; for thy loving-kindness is good:
   Turn unto me according to the multitude of thy tender mercies.
And hide not thy face from thy servant;
   For I am in trouble: hear me speedily.
Draw nigh unto my soul, and redeem it:
   Deliver me, because of mine enemies.
Thou hast known my reproach, and my shame, and my dishonor:
   Mine adversaries are all before thee.
Reproach hath broken my heart; and I am full of heaviness:
   { *And I looked for some to take pity, but there was none;*
   { *And for comforters, but I found none.*
They gave me also gall for my meat;
   And in my thirst they gave me vinegar to drink.

But I am poor and sorrowful :
  Let thy salvation, O God, set me up on high.
I will praise the name of God with a song,
  And will magnify him with thanksgiving.
This also shall please the LORD,
  Better than an ox or bullock that hath horns and hoofs.
The humble shall see this, and be glad :
  And your heart shall live that seek God.
For the LORD heareth the poor,
  And despiseth not his prisoners.
Let the heaven and earth praise him,
  The seas, and every thing that moveth therein.
For God will save Zion, and will build the cities of Judah :
  That they may dwell there, and have it in possession.
The seed also of his servants shall inherit it :
  And they that love his name shall dwell therein.

PSALM LXX.

MAKE haste, O God, to deliver me ;
  Make haste to help me, O LORD.
{ Let them be ashamed and confounded
{ That seek after my soul :
  { *Let them be turned backward, and put to confusion,*
  { *That desire my hurt.*
Let them be turned back for a reward of their shame
  That say, Aha! aha!
{ Let all those that seek thee
{ Rejoice and be glad in thee :
  { *And let such as love thy salvation*
  { *Say continually, Let God be magnified.*
{ But I am poor and needy :
{ Make haste unto me, O God :
  { *Thou art my help and my deliverer ;*
  { *O* LORD, *make no tarrying.*

Lesson 60. (Page 128.)

From Psalm LXXIV.

O GOD, why hast thou cast us off for ever?
    Why doth thine anger smoke against the sheep of thy pasture?
Remember thy congregation, which thou hast purchased of old;
    The rod of thine inheritance, which thou hast redeemed; this mount Zion, wherein thou hast dwelt.
Lift up thy feet unto the perpetual desolations;
    Even all that the enemy hath done wickedly in the sanctuary.
A man was famous according as he had lifted up axes upon the thick trees.
    But now they break down the carved work thereof at once with axes and hammers.
They have cast fire into thy sanctuary,
    They have defiled by casting down the dwelling-place of thy name to the ground.
They said in their hearts, Let us destroy them together:
    They have burned up all the synagogues of God in the land.
We see not our signs:
    There is no more any prophet: neither is there among us any that knoweth how long!
O God, how long shall the adversary reproach?
    Shall the enemy blaspheme thy name for ever?
Why withdrawest thou thy hand, even thy right hand?
    Pluck it out of thy bosom.
For God is my King of old,
    Working salvation in the midst of the earth.
Thou didst divide the sea by thy strength:
    Thou brakest the heads of the dragons in the waters.
Thou brakest the heads of leviathan in pieces,
    And gavest him to be meat to the people inhabiting the wilderness.
Thou didst cleave the fountain and the flood:
    Thou driedst up mighty rivers.
The day is thine, the night also is thine:
    Thou hast prepared the light and the sun.
Thou hast set all the borders of the earth:
    Thou hast made summer and winter.
Remember this, that the enemy hath reproached, O LORD,
    And that the foolish people have blasphemed thy name.

Have respect unto the covenant :
For the dark places of the earth are full of the habitations of cruelty.
Oh let not the oppressed return ashamed :
Let the poor and needy praise thy name.

FROM PSALM XCIV.

O LORD God, to whom vengeance belongeth ;
O God, to whom vengeance belongeth, show thyself.
Lift up thyself, thou judge of the earth :
Render a reward to the proud.
LORD, how long shall the wicked,
How long shall the wicked triumph?
How long shall they utter and speak hard things?
And all the workers of iniquity boast themselves?
They break in pieces thy people, O LORD,
And afflict thine heritage.
They slay the widow and the stranger,
And murder the fatherless.
Yet they say, The LORD shall not see,
Neither shall the God of Jacob regard it.
He that planted the ear, shall he not hear?
He that formed the eye, shall he not see?
He that chastiseth the heathen, shall not he correct?
He that teacheth man knowledge, shall not he know?
The LORD knoweth the thoughts of man, that they are vanity,
Blessed is the man whom thou chastenest, O LORD, and teachest him out of thy law ;
That thou mayest give him rest from the days of adversity,
Until the pit be digged for the wicked.
For the LORD will not cast off his people,
Neither will he forsake his inheritance.
But judgment shall return unto righteousness :
And all the upright in heart shall follow it.
Unless the LORD had been my help, my soul had almost dwelt in silence.
When I said, My foot slippeth : thy mercy, O LORD, held me up.
In the multitude of my thoughts within me thy comforts delight my soul.
Shall the throne of iniquity have fellowship with thee, which frameth mischief by a law?
They gather themselves together against the soul of the righteous,
And condemn the innocent blood.
But the LORD is my defence ;
And my God is the rock of my refuge.

[The following Selections from different parts of the Scriptures, in which the poetical structure appears, and which are intrinsically adapted to responsive reading or to antiphonal singing, will be found, it is hoped, not only suitable for use in the same way with the Psalms in public worship, but helpful through such use to the spirit of congregations: whether for instruction or the office of praise, for the quickening of humility, or for the lifting up of faithful hearts in holy hope.]

Lesson 61. (Page 130.)

1 Chronicles XVI : 8—36.

(David's Psalm of Thanksgiving for the Ark.)

GIVE thanks unto the Lord, call upon his name,
 Make known his deeds among the people.
Sing unto him, sing psalms unto him,
 Talk ye of all his wondrous works.
Glory ye in his holy name;
 Let the heart of them rejoice that seek the Lord.
Seek the Lord and his strength,
 Seek his face continually.
Remember his marvellous works that he hath done,
 His wonders, and the judgments of his mouth;
O ye seed of Israel his servant,
 Ye children of Jacob, his chosen ones.
He is the Lord our God;
 His judgments are in all the earth.
Be ye mindful always of his covenant;
 The word which he commanded to a thousand generations;
Even of the covenant which he made with Abraham,
 And of his oath unto Isaac;
And hath confirmed the same to Jacob for a law,
 And to Israel for an everlasting covenant,
Saying, Unto thee will I give the land of Canaan,
 The lot of your inheritance;
When ye were but few,
 Even a few, and strangers in it.
And when they went from nation to nation,
 And from one kingdom to another people,
He suffered no man to do them wrong:
 Yea, he reproved kings for their sakes,

Saying, Touch not mine anointed,
And do my prophets no harm.
Sing unto the LORD, all the earth;
Show forth from day to day his salvation.
Declare his glory among the heathen;
His marvellous works among all nations.
For great is the LORD, and greatly to be praised:
He also is to be feared above all gods.
For all the gods of the people are idols;
But the LORD *made the heavens.*
Glory and honor are in his presence;
Strength and gladness are in his place.
Give unto the LORD, ye kindreds of the people,
Give unto the LORD *glory and strength.*
Give unto the LORD the glory due unto his name:
{ *Bring an offering, and come before him:*
{ *Worship the* LORD *in the beauty of holiness.*
Fear before him, all the earth:
The world also shall be stable, that it be not moved.
Let the heavens be glad, and let the earth rejoice:
And let men say among the nations, The LORD *reigneth.*
Let the sea roar, and the fulness thereof:
Let the fields rejoice, and all that is therein.
Then shall the trees of the wood sing out
At the presence of the LORD, *because he cometh to judge the earth.*
O give thanks unto the LORD; for he is good;
For his mercy endureth for ever.
And say ye, Save us, O God of our salvation,
And gather us together, and deliver us from the heathen,
That we may give thanks to thy holy name, and glory in thy praise.
Blessed be the LORD *God of Israel, for ever and ever!*

Lesson 62. (Page 132.)

From Deuteronomy XXXIII.

(The Blessing of Moses.)

THE LORD came from Sinai,
    And rose up from Seir unto them:
He shined forth from mount Paran,
    { *And he came with ten thousands of saints:*
    { *From his right hand went a fiery law for them.*
{ Yea, he loved the people;
{ All his saints are in thy hand:
    { *And they sat down at thy feet;*
    { *Every one shall receive of thy words.*
Moses commanded us a law,
    Even the inheritance of the congregation of Jacob.
And he was king in Jeshurun,
    { *When the heads of the people*
    { *And the tribes of Israel were gathered together.*
Let Reuben live, and not die;
    And let not his men be few.
And this is the blessing of Judah:
    And he said, Hear, LORD, the voice of Judah,
And bring him unto his people:
    { *Let his hands be sufficient for him;*
    { *And be thou an help to him from his enemies.*
And of Levi he said,
    Let thy Thummim and thy Urim be with thy holy one.
Whom thou didst prove at Massah,
    And with whom thou didst strive at the waters of Meribah;
Who said unto his father and to his mother, I have not seen him:
    { *Neither did he acknowledge his brethren,*
    { *Nor knew his own children:*
For they have observed thy word,
    And kept thy covenant.
{ They shall teach Jacob thy judgments,
{ And Israel thy law:
    { *They shall put incense before thee,*
    { *And whole burnt sacrifice upon thine altar.*

And of Benjamin he said,
The beloved of the LORD *shall dwell in safety by him ;*
And the LORD shall cover him all the day long,
And he shall dwell between his shoulders.
And of Joseph he said,
Blessed of the LORD *be his land,*
For the precious things of heaven,
For the dew, and for the deep that coucheth beneath,
And for the precious fruits brought forth by the sun,
And for the precious things put forth by the moon,
And for the chief things of the ancient mountains,
And for the precious things of the lasting hills,
And for the precious things of the earth and fulness thereof,
And for the good-will of him that dwelt in the bush :
Let the blessing come upon the head of Joseph,
And upon the top of the head of him that was separated from his brethren.
His glory is like the firstling of his bullock,
And his horns are like the horns of unicorns :
With them he shall push the people together, to the ends of the earth :
{ *And they are the ten thousands of Ephraim,*
{ *And they are the thousands of Manasseh.*
There is none like unto the God of Jeshurun,
{ *Who rideth upon the heaven in thy help,*
{ *And in his excellency on the sky.*
The eternal God is thy refuge,
And underneath are the everlasting arms :
And he shall thrust out the enemy from before thee ;
And shall say, Destroy them.
Israel then shall dwell in safety alone :
{ *The fountain of Jacob shall be upon a land of corn and wine ;*
{ *Also his heavens shall drop down dew.*
Happy art thou, O Israel :
{ *Who is like unto thee, O people saved by the* LORD,
{ *The shield of thy help, and who is the sword of thy excellency !*
And thine enemies shall be found liars unto thee ;
And thou shalt tread upon their high places.

Lesson 63. (Page 134.)

From Exodus XV.

(The Song of Moses.)

I WILL sing unto the Lord, for he hath triumphed gloriously:
 The horse and his rider hath he thrown into the sea.
The Lord is my strength and song,
 And he is become my salvation:
He is my God, and I will prepare him an habitation;
 My father's God, and I will exalt him.
The Lord is a man of war:
 The Lord is his name:
Pharaoh's chariots, and his host, hath he cast into the sea:
 His chosen captains also are drowned in the Red Sea.
The depths have covered them:
 They sank unto the bottom as a stone.
Thy right hand, O Lord, is become glorious in power:
 Thy right hand, O Lord, hath dashed in pieces the enemy.
And in the greatness of thine excellency thou hast overthrown them that rose up against thee:
 Thou sentest forth thy wrath, which consumed them as stubble.
And with the blast of thy nostrils the waters were gathered together,
 { *The floods stood upright as a heap,*
 { *And the depths were congealed in the heart of the sea.*
The enemy said, I will pursue, I will overtake,
 { *I will divide the spoil; my lust shall be satisfied upon them;*
 { *I will draw my sword, my hand shall destroy them.*
Thou didst blow with thy wind, the sea covered them:
 They sank as lead in the mighty waters.
Who is like unto thee, O Lord, among the gods?
 { *Who is like thee, glorious in holiness,*
 { *Fearful in praises, doing wonders?*
Thou stretchedst out thy right hand,
 The earth swallowed them.
Thou in thy mercy hast led forth the people which thou hast redeemed:
 Thou hast guided them in thy strength, unto thy holy habitation.
The people shall hear, and be afraid:
 Sorrow shall take hold on the inhabitants of Palestina.

Then the dukes of Edom shall be amazed;
  { The mighty men of Moab, trembling shall take hold upon them;
  { All the inhabitants of Canaan shall melt away.
  { Fear and dread shall fall upon them:
  { By the greatness of thine arm they shall be as still as a stone;
  { Till thy people pass over, O LORD,
  { Till the people pass over, which thou hast purchased.
Thou shalt bring them in, and plant them in the mountain of thine inheritance.
  In the place, O LORD, which thou hast made for thee to dwell in,
In the sanctuary, O LORD, which thy hands have established.
  The LORD shall reign for ever and ever.
And Miriam the prophetess, the sister of Aaron, took a timbrel in her hand;
  And all the women went out after her, with timbrels and with dances.
  { And Miriam answered them,
  { Sing ye to the LORD, for he hath triumphed gloriously;
  The horse and his rider hath he thrown into the sea.

Lesson 64. (PAGE 135.)

FROM NUMBERS XXIII, XXIV.

(The commanded Prophecies of Balaam.)

HOW shall I curse, whom God hath not cursed?
  Or how shall I defy, whom the LORD hath not defied?
For from the top of the rocks I see him,
  And from the hills I behold him:
Lo, the people shall dwell alone,
  And shall not be reckoned among the nations.
Who can count the dust of Jacob,
  And the number of the fourth part of Israel?
Let me die the death of the righteous,
  And let my last end be like his!
God is not a man, that he should lie;
  Neither the son of man, that he should repent:
Hath he said—and shall he not do it?
  Or hath he spoken—and shall he not make it good?
Behold, I have received commandment to bless:
  And he hath blessed; and I cannot reverse it.

He hath not beheld iniquity in Jacob,
>Neither hath he seen perverseness in Israel:
The LORD his God is with him,
>And the shout of a king is among them.
God brought them out of Egypt;
>He hath as it were the strength of an unicorn.
Surely there is no enchantment against Jacob,
>Neither is there any divination against Israel:
According to this time it shall be said of Jacob
>And of Israel, What hath God wrought!
He hath said, which heard the words of God,
>{ Which saw the vision of the Almighty,
>{ Falling into a trance, but having his eyes open:
How goodly are thy tents, O Jacob!
>And thy tabernacles, O Israel!
As the valleys are they spread forth,
>As gardens by the river's side,
As the trees of lign aloes which the LORD hath planted,
>And as cedar trees beside the waters.
He shall pour the water out of his buckets,
>And his seed shall be in many waters,
And his king shall be higher than Agag,
>And his kingdom shall be exalted.
God brought him forth out of Egypt;
>He hath as it were the strength of an unicorn:
He shall eat up the nations his enemies,
>{ And shall break their bones,
>{ And pierce them through with his arrows.
He couched, he lay down as a lion,
>And as a great lion: who shall stir him up?
Blessed is he that blesseth thee,
>And cursed is he that curseth thee.
He hath said, which heard the words of God,
>And knew the knowledge of the Most High,
Which saw the vision of the Almighty,
>Falling into a trance, but having his eyes open:
I shall see him—but not now:
>I shall behold him—but not nigh:
There shall come a Star out of Jacob,
>And a Sceptre shall rise out of Israel,
And shall smite the corners of Moab,
>And destroy all the children of Sheth.

And Edom shall be a possession,
  { Seir also shall be a possession for his enemies;
  { And Israel shall do valiantly.
Out of Jacob shall come he that shall have dominion,
  And shall destroy him that remaineth of the city.

Lesson 65. (Page 137.)

Habakkuk III.

O LORD, I have heard thy speech, and was afraid:
  O LORD, revive thy work in the midst of the years,
In the midst of the years make known;
  In wrath remember mercy.
God came from Teman,
  And the Holy One from mount Paran.
His glory covered the heavens,
  And the earth was full of his praise.
And his brightness was as the light;
  { He had horns coming out of his hand:
  { And there was the hiding of his power.
Before him went the pestilence,
  And burning coals went forth at his feet.
He stood, and measured the earth:
  He beheld, and drove asunder the nations;
And the everlasting mountains were scattered,
  The perpetual hills did bow; his ways are everlasting.
I saw the tents of Cushan in affliction:
  And the curtains of the land of Midian did tremble.
Was the LORD displeased against the rivers?
  Was thine anger against the rivers?
Was thy wrath against the sea,
  That thou didst ride upon thine horses, and thy chariots of salvation?
{ Thy bow was made quite naked,
{ According to the oaths of the tribes, even thy word.
  Thou didst cleave the earth with rivers.
The mountains saw thee, and they trembled:
  The overflowing of the water passed by:

The deep uttered his voice,
And lifted up his hands on high.
The sun and moon stood still in their habitation:
{ *At the light of thine arrows they went,*
And at the shining of thy glittering spear.
Thou didst march through the land in indignation:
Thou didst thresh the heathen in anger.
Thou wentest forth for the salvation of thy people,
Even for salvation with thine anointed;
Thou woundedst the head out of the house of the wicked,
By discovering the foundation unto the neck.
Thou didst strike through with his staves the head of his villages;
{ *They came out as a whirlwind to scatter me:*
Their rejoicing was as to devour the poor secretly.
Thou didst walk through the sea with thine horses,
Through the heap of great waters.
When I heard, my belly trembled;
My lips quivered at the voice:
Rottenness entered into my bones, and I trembled in myself,
{ *That I might rest in the day of trouble:*
When he cometh up unto the people, he will invade them with his troops.
Although the fig tree shall not blossom,
Neither shall fruit be in the vines;
The labor of the olive shall fail,
And the fields shall yield no meat;
The flock shall be cut off from the fold,
And there shall be no herd in the stalls:
Yet I will rejoice in the LORD,
I will joy in the God of my salvation.
The LORD God is my strength,
{ *And he will make my feet like hinds' feet,*
And he will make me to walk upon mine high places.

Lesson 66. (Page 139.)

Job XXXVI : 26—32.

BEHOLD, God is great, and we know him not,
Neither can the number of his years be searched out.
For he maketh small the drops of water:
They pour down rain according to the vapor thereof:
Which the clouds do drop,
And distil upon man abundantly.
Also can any understand the spreadings of the clouds,
Or the noise of his tabernacle?
Behold, he spreadeth his light upon it,
And covereth the bottom of the sea.
For by them judgeth he the people;
He giveth meat in abundance.
With clouds he covereth the light;
And commandeth it not to shine by the cloud that cometh betwixt.

Job XXXVII.

AT this also my heart trembleth,
And is moved out of his place.
Hear attentively the noise of his voice,
And the sound that goeth out of his mouth.
He directeth it under the whole heaven,
And his lightning unto the ends of the earth.
After it a voice roareth:
{ *He thundereth with the voice of his excellency;*
{ *And he will not stay them when his voice is heard.*
God thundereth marvellously with his voice;
Great things doeth he, which we cannot comprehend.
For he saith to the snow, Be thou on the earth;
Likewise to the small rain, and to the great rain of his strength.
He sealeth up the hand of every man;
That all men may know his work.
Then the beasts go into dens,
And remain in their places.
Out of the south cometh the whirlwind:
And cold out of the north.

By the breath of God frost is given:
And the breadth of the waters is straitened.
Also by watering he wearieth the thick cloud:
He scattereth his bright cloud:
And it is turned round about by his counsels:
{ *That they may do whatsoever he commandeth them*
{ *Upon the face of the world in the earth.*
He causeth it to come,
Whether for correction, or for his land, or for mercy.
Hearken unto this, O Job:
Stand still, and consider the wondrous works of God.
Dost thou know when God disposed them,
And caused the light of his cloud to shine?
Dost thou know the balancings of the clouds,
The wondrous works of him which is perfect in knowledge?
How thy garments are warm,
When he quieteth the earth by the south wind?
Hast thou with him spread out the sky,
Which is strong, and as a molten looking glass?
Teach us what we shall say unto him;
For we cannot order our speech by reason of darkness.
Shall it be told him that I speak?
If a man speak, surely he shall be swallowed up.
And now men see not the bright light which is in the clouds:
But the wind passeth, and cleanseth them.
Fair weather cometh out of the north:
With God is terrible majesty.
Touching the Almighty, we cannot find him out:
{ *He is excellent in power, and in judgment,*
{ *And in plenty of justice: he will not afflict.*
Men do therefore fear him:
He respecteth not any that are wise of heart.

Lesson 67. (Page 141.)

From Job XXXVIII; XL.

WHO is this that darkeneth counsel
  By words without knowledge?
Gird up now thy loins like a man;
  For I will demand of thee, and answer thou me.
Where wast thou when I laid the foundations of the earth?
  Declare, if thou hast understanding.
Who hath laid the measures thereof, if thou knowest?
  Or who hath stretched the line upon it?
Whereupon are the foundations thereof fastened?
  Or who laid the corner stone thereof;
When the morning stars sang together,
  And all the sons of God shouted for joy?
Or who shut up the sea with doors,
  When it brake forth, as if it had issued out of the womb?
When I made the cloud the garment thereof,
  And thick darkness a swaddling-band for it,
And brake up for it my decreed place:
  And set bars and doors,
And said, Hitherto shalt thou come, but no further:
  And here shall thy proud waves be stayed?
Hast thou commanded the morning since thy days;
  And caused the dayspring to know his place;
That it might take hold of the ends of the earth,
  That the wicked might be shaken out of it?
It is turned as clay to the seal;
  And they stand as a garment.
And from the wicked their light is withholden,
  And the high arm shall be broken.
Hast thou entered into the springs of the sea?
  Or hast thou walked in the search of the depth?
Have the gates of death been opened unto thee?
  Or hast thou seen the doors of the shadow of death?
Hast thou perceived the breadth of the earth?
  Declare if thou knowest it all.
Where is the way where light dwelleth?
  And as for darkness, where is the place thereof,

That thou shouldest take it to the bound thereof,
And that thou shouldest know the paths to the house thereof?
Knowest thou it, because thou wast then born?
Or because the number of thy days is great?
Hast thou entered into the treasures of the snow?
Or hast thou seen the treasures of the hail,
Which I have reserved against the time of trouble,
Against the day of battle and war?
By what way is the light parted,
Which scattereth the east wind upon the earth?
Who hath divided a watercourse for the overflowing of waters,
Or a way for the lightning of thunder;
To cause it to rain on the earth, where no man is;
On the wilderness, wherein there is no man;
To satisfy the desolate and waste ground;
And to cause the bud of the tender herb to spring forth!
Hath the rain a father?
Or who hath begotten the drops of dew?
Out of whose womb came the ice?
And the hoary frost of heaven, who hath gendered it?
The waters are hid as with a stone,
And the face of the deep is frozen.
Canst thou bind the sweet influences of Pleiades,
Or loose the bands of Orion?
Canst thou bring forth Mazzaroth in his season?
Or canst thou guide Arcturus with his sons?
Knowest thou the ordinances of heaven?
Canst thou set the dominion thereof in the earth?
Canst thou lift up thy voice to the clouds,
That abundance of waters may cover thee?
Canst thou send lightnings, that they may go,
And say unto thee, Here we are?
Who hath put wisdom in the inward parts?
Or who hath given understanding to the heart?
Who can number the clouds in wisdom?
Or who can stay the bottles of heaven,
When the dust groweth into hardness,
And the clods cleave fast together?
Shall he that contendeth with the Almighty instruct him?
He that reproveth God, let him answer it.

Lesson 68. (Page 142.)

Isaiah XI : 1—9.

AND there shall come forth a rod out of the stem of Jesse,
And a Branch shall grow out of his roots:
And the Spirit of the LORD shall rest upon him,
The spirit of wisdom and understanding,
The spirit of counsel and might,
The spirit of knowledge and of the fear of the LORD;
And shall make him of quick understanding,
In the fear of the LORD:
And he shall not judge after the sight of his eyes,
Neither reprove after the hearing of his ears:
But with righteousness shall he judge the poor,
And reprove with equity for the meek of the earth.
And he shall smite the earth with the rod of his mouth,
And with the breath of his lips shall he slay the wicked.
And righteousness shall be the girdle of his loins,
And faithfulness the girdle of his reins.
The wolf also shall dwell with the lamb,
And the leopard shall lie down with the kid;
And the calf, and the young lion, and the fatling together;
And a little child shall lead them.
And the cow and the bear shall feed; their young ones shall lie down together;
And the lion shall eat straw like the ox.
And the sucking child shall play on the hole of the asp,
And the weaned child shall put his hand on the cockatrice' den.
They shall not hurt nor destroy in all my holy mountain,
For the earth shall be full of the knowledge of the LORD, *as the waters cover the sea.*

Isaiah XLII : 1—12.

BEHOLD my servant, whom I uphold;
Mine elect, in whom my soul delighteth;
I have put my Spirit upon him;
He shall bring forth judgment to the Gentiles.
He shall not cry, nor lift up,
Nor cause his voice to be heard in the street.
A bruised reed shall he not break, and the smoking flax shall he not quench:
He shall bring forth judgment unto truth.

He shall not fail nor be discouraged, till he have set judgment in the earth:
And the isles shall wait for his law.
Thus saith God the LORD,
He that created the heavens, and stretched them out;
He that spread forth the earth,
And that which cometh out of it;
He that giveth breath unto the people upon it,
And spirit to them that walk therein:
I the LORD have called thee in righteousness,
And will hold thine hand, and will keep thee,
And give thee for a covenant of the people,
For a light of the Gentiles;
To open the blind eyes, to bring out the prisoners from the prison,
And them that sit in darkness, out of the prison-house.
I am the LORD: that is my name: and my glory will I not give to another,
Neither my praise to graven images.
Behold the former things are come to pass, and new things do I declare:
Before they spring forth I tell you of them.
Sing unto the LORD a new song,
And his praise from the end of the earth,
Ye that go down to the sea, and all that is therein;
The isles, and the inhabitants thereof.
Let the wilderness and the cities thereof lift up their voice,
The villages that Kedar doth inhabit:
Let the inhabitants of the rock sing,
Let them shout from the top of the mountains.
Let them give glory unto the LORD,
And declare his praise in the islands.

Lesson 69. (PAGE 144.)

ISAIAH LXI : 1—7.

THE Spirit of the LORD GOD is upon me;
Because the LORD hath anointed me to preach good tidings unto the meek;
He hath sent me to bind up the broken-hearted,
{ *To proclaim liberty to the captives,*
{ *And the opening of the prison to them that are bound.*

{ To proclaim the acceptable year of the LORD,
{ And the day of vengeance of our God ;
   To comfort all that mourn ;
To appoint unto them that mourn in Zion,
   To give unto them beauty for ashes,
The oil of joy for mourning,
   The garment of praise for the spirit of heaviness ;
That they might be called trees of righteousness ;
   The planting of the LORD, that he might be glorified.
And they shall build the old wastes,
   They shall raise up the former desolations,
And they shall repair the waste cities,
   The desolations of many generations.
And strangers shall stand and feed your flocks,
   And the sons of the alien shall be your ploughmen and your vine-dressers.
But ye shall be named the Priests of the LORD :
   Men shall call you the Ministers of our God :
Ye shall eat the riches of the Gentiles,
   And in their glory shall ye boast yourselves.
For your shame ye shall have double ;
   And for confusion they shall rejoice in their portion ;
Therefore in their land they shall possess the double :
   Everlasting joy shall be upon them.

ISAIAH LV : 1—13.

HO, every one that thirsteth, come ye to the waters,
   And he that hath no money : come ye, buy, and eat :
Yea, come, buy wine and milk,
   Without money and without price.
Wherefore do ye spend money for that which is not bread ?
   And your labor for that which satisfieth not ?
Hearken diligently unto me, and eat ye that which is good,
   And let your soul delight itself in fatness.
Incline your ear, and come unto me;
   Hear, and your soul shall live :
And I will make an everlasting covenant with you,
   Even the sure mercies of David.
Behold, I have given him for a witness to the people,
   A leader and commander to the people.
Behold, thou shalt call a nation that thou knowest not,
   And nations that knew not thee shall run unto thee,

Because of the LORD thy God, and for the Holy One of Israel;
For he hath glorified thee.
Seek ye the LORD while he may be found,
Call ye upon him while he is near:
Let the wicked forsake his way,
And the unrighteous man his thoughts:
And let him return unto the LORD, and he will have mercy upon him:
And to our God, for he will abundantly pardon.
For my thoughts are not your thoughts,
Neither are your ways my ways, saith the LORD.
For as the heavens are higher than the earth,
{ *So are my ways higher than your ways,*
{ *And my thoughts than your thoughts.*
For as the rain cometh down, and the snow from heaven,
And returneth not thither,
But watereth the earth, and maketh it bring forth, and bud,
That it may give seed to the sower, and bread to the eater:
So shall my word be that goeth forth out of my mouth;
It shall not return unto me void,
But it shall accomplish that which I please,
And it shall prosper in the thing whereto I sent it.
For ye shall go out with joy,
And be led forth with peace:
The mountains and the hills shall break forth before you into singing,
And all the trees of the field shall clap their hands.
Instead of the thorn shall come up the fir tree,
And instead of the brier shall come up the myrtle tree:
And it shall be to the LORD for a name,
For an everlasting sign that shall not be cut off.

Lesson 70. (PAGE 146.)

ISAIAH LIII; LII : 12—15.

WHO hath believed our report?
And to whom is the arm of the LORD *revealed?*
For he shall grow up before him as a tender plant,
And as a root out of a dry ground:

He hath no form nor comeliness;
> And when we shall see him,
> There is no beauty that we should desire him.

He is despised and rejected of men;
> A man of sorrows, and acquainted with grief:

And we hid as it were our faces from him;
> He was despised, and we esteemed him not.

Surely he hath borne our griefs, and carried our sorrows:
> Yet we did esteem him stricken, smitten of God, and afflicted.

But he was wounded for our transgressions,
> He was bruised for our iniquities:

The chastisement of our peace was upon him;
> And with his stripes we are healed.

All we like sheep have gone astray;
> We have turned every one to his own way;
> And the LORD hath laid on him the iniquity of us all.

He was oppressed, and he was afflicted,
> Yet he opened not his mouth:

He is brought as a lamb to the slaughter,
> And as a sheep before her shearers is dumb,
> So he openeth not his mouth.

He was taken from prison and from judgment:
And who shall declare his generation:
> For he was cut off out of the land of the living:
> For the transgression of my people was he stricken.

And he made his grave with the wicked,
> And with the rich in his death;

Because he had done no violence,
> Neither was any deceit in his mouth.

Yet it pleased the LORD to bruise him;
> He hath put him to grief:

When thou shalt make his soul an offering for sin,
> He shall see his seed, he shall prolong his days,
> And the pleasure of the LORD shall prosper in his hand.

He shall see of the travail of his soul, and shall be satisfied:
> By his knowledge shall my righteous servant justify many;
> For he shall bear their iniquities.

Therefore will I divide him a portion with the great,
> And he shall divide the spoil with the strong;

Because he hath poured out his soul unto death;
> And he was numbered with the transgressors;

And he bare the sin of many,
> And made intercession for the transgressors.

Behold, my servant shall deal prudently,
He shall be exalted and extolled, and be very high.
As many were astonished at thee :
{ *His visage was so marred more than any man,*
{ *And his form more than the sons of men :*
So shall he sprinkle many nations ;
The kings shall shut their mouths at him :
For that which had not been told them shall they see :
And that which they had not heard shall they consider.

Lesson 71. (Page 148.)

From Isaiah IX; XII; XXXV.

THE people that walked in darkness, have seen a great light:
They that dwell in the land of the shadow of death, upon them hath the light shined.
For unto us a child is born, unto us a son is given :
And the government shall be upon his shoulder :
And his name shall be called Wonderful, Counsellor.
The mighty God, the everlasting Father, the Prince of Peace.
Of the increase of his government and peace there shall be no end.
Upon the throne of David, and upon his kingdom ;
{ To order it, and to establish it
{ With judgment and with justice, from henceforth even for ever.
The zeal of the Lord of hosts will perform this.
And in that day thou shalt say, O Lord, I will praise thee :
{ *Though thou wast angry with me, thine anger is turned away,*
{ *And thou comfortedst me.*
Behold, God is my salvation ;
I will trust, and not be afraid :
For the Lord Jehovah is my strength and my song ;
He also is become my salvation.
Therefore with joy shall ye draw water out of the wells of salvation.
And in that day shall ye say, Praise the Lord.
Call upon his name, declare his doings among the people,
Make mention that his name is exalted.
Sing unto the Lord ; for he hath done excellent things:
This is known in all the earth.

Cry out and shout, thou inhabitant of Zion:
 For great is the Holy One of Israel in the midst of thee.
The wilderness and the solitary place shall be glad for them;
 And the desert shall rejoice, and blossom as the rose.
{ It shall blossom abundantly,
{ And rejoice even with joy and singing:
 { *The glory of Lebanon shall be given unto it,*
 { *The excellency of Carmel and Sharon.*
They shall see the glory of the LORD,
 And the excellency of our God.
Strengthen ye the weak hands,
 And confirm the feeble knees.
Say to them that are of a fearful heart, Be strong, fear not:
 { *Behold, your God will come with vengeance,*
 { *Even God with a recompence; he will come, and save you.*
Then the eyes of the blind shall be opened,
 And the ears of the deaf shall be unstopped.
Then shall the lame man leap as an hart,
 And the tongue of the dumb sing:
For in the wilderness shall waters break out,
 And streams in the desert.
{ And the parched ground shall become a pool,
{ And the thirsty land springs of water:
 { *In the habitation of dragons, where each lay,*
 { *Shall be grass with reeds and rushes.*
And an highway shall be there, and a way,
 And it shall be called The way of holiness;
The unclean shall not pass over it; but it shall be for those:
 The wayfaring men, though fools, shall not err therein.
{ No lion shall be there,
{ Nor any ravenous beast shall go up thereon,
 { *It shall not be found there;*
 { *But the redeemed shall walk there:*
And the ransomed of the LORD shall return,
 { *And come to Zion with songs*
 { *And everlasting joy upon their heads:*
They shall obtain joy and gladness,
 And sorrow and sighing shall flee away.

Lesson 72. (Page 150.)

From Isaiah XL.

COMFORT ye, comfort ye my people, saith your God.
  Speak ye comfortably to Jerusalem,
And cry unto her, that her warfare is accomplished,
  { *That her iniquity is pardoned,*
  { *For she hath received of the* LORD'*s hand double for all her sins.*
The voice of him that crieth in the wilderness,
  { *Prepare ye the way of the* LORD,
  { *Make straight in the desert a highway for our God.*
Every valley shall be exalted,
  And every mountain and hill shall be made low;
And the crooked shall be made straight,
  And the rough places plain:
And the glory of the LORD shall be revealed,
  { *And all flesh shall see it together:*
  { *For the mouth of the* LORD *hath spoken it.*
The voice said, Cry.
  And he said, What shall I cry?
All flesh is grass,
  And all the goodliness thereof is as the flower of the field:
The grass withereth, the flower fadeth:
  Because the spirit of the LORD *bloweth upon it: surely the people is grass.*
The grass withereth, the flower fadeth:
  But the word of our God shall stand for ever.
O Zion, that bringest good tidings, get thee up into the high mountain;
  O Jerusalem, that bringest good tidings, lift up thy voice with strength;
Lift it up, be not afraid;
  Say unto the cities of Judah, Behold your God!
Behold, the LORD GOD will come with strong hand,
  And his arm shall rule for him:
Behold, his reward is with him,
  And his work before him.
He shall feed his flock like a shepherd:
  He shall gather the lambs with his arm,
And carry them in his bosom,
  And shall gently lead those that are with young.

Who hath measured the waters in the hollow of his hand,
And meted out heaven with the span,
And comprehended the dust of the earth in a measure,
And weighed the mountains in scales, and the hills in a balance?
Who hath directed the Spirit of the LORD,
Or being his counsellor hath taught him?
It is he that sitteth upon the circle of the earth,
And the inhabitants thereof are as grasshoppers;
That stretcheth out the heavens as a curtain,
And spreadeth them out as a tent to dwell in:
That bringeth the princes to nothing;
He maketh the judges of the earth as vanity.
Yea, they shall not be planted; yea, they shall not be sown:
Yea, their stock shall not take root in the earth:
And he shall also blow upon them, and they shall wither,
And the whirlwind shall take them away as stubble.
To whom then will ye liken me,
Or shall I be equal? saith the Holy One.
Lift up your eyes on high, and behold who hath created these things,
That bringeth out their host by number:
He calleth them all by names, by the greatness of his might,
For that he is strong in power; not one faileth.
Why sayest thou, O Jacob,
And speakest, O Israel,
My way is hid from the LORD,
And my judgment is passed over from my God?
Hast thou not known? hast thou not heard, that the everlasting God,
The LORD, the Creator of the ends of the earth,
Fainteth not, neither is weary?
There is no searching of his understanding.
He giveth power to the faint;
And to them that have no might he increaseth strength.
Even the youths shall faint and be weary,
And the young men shall utterly fall:
But they that wait upon the LORD shall renew their strength;
They shall mount up with wings as eagles;
They shall run, and not be weary;
And they shall walk, and not faint.

Lesson 73. (Page 152.)

From Isaiah LX.

ARISE, shine: for thy light is come,
    And the glory of the Lord *is risen upon thee.*
For, behold, the darkness shall cover the earth,
    And gross darkness the people:
But the Lord shall arise upon thee,
    And his glory shall be seen upon thee.
And the Gentiles shall come to thy light,
    And kings to the brightness of thy rising.
Lift up thine eyes round about, and see:
    All they gather themselves together, they come to thee:
Thy sons shall come from far,
    And thy daughters shall be nursed at thy side.
Then thou shalt see, and flow together,
    And thine heart shall fear and be enlarged;
Because the abundance of the sea shall be converted unto thee,
    The forces of the Gentiles shall come unto thee.
{ The multitude of camels shall come unto thee,
{ The dromedaries of Midian and Ephah;
    All they from Sheba shall come:
They shall bring gold and incense:
    And they shall show forth the praises of the Lord.
All the flocks of Kedar shall be gathered together unto thee,
    The rams of Nebaioth shall minister unto thee:
They shall come up with acceptance on mine altar,
    And I will glorify the house of my glory.
Who are these that fly as a cloud,
    And as the doves to their windows?
Surely the isles shall wait for me, and the ships of Tarshish first,
    To bring thy sons from far, their silver and their gold with them.
Unto the name of the Lord thy God,
    And to the Holy One of Israel, because he hath glorified thee.
And the sons of strangers shall build up thy walls,
    And their kings shall minister unto thee;
For in my wrath I smote thee,
    But in my favor have I had mercy on thee.

Therefore thy gates shall be open continually ;
They shall not be shut day nor night ;
That men may bring unto thee the forces of the Gentiles,
And that their kings may be brought.
For the nation and kingdom that will not serve thee shall perish :
Yea, those nations shall be utterly wasted.
The glory of Lebanon shall come unto thee,
The fir tree, the pine tree, and the box together,
To beautify the place of my sanctuary ;
And I will make the place of my feet glorious.
The sons also of them that afflicted thee shall come bending unto thee
And all they that despised thee shall bow themselves down at the soles of thy feet ;
And they shall call thee The city of the LORD,
The Zion of the Holy One of Israel.
Whereas thou hast been forsaken and hated,
So that no man went through thee,
I will make thee an eternal excellency,
A joy of many generations.
Thou shalt also suck the milk of the Gentiles,
And shalt suck the breast of kings :
And thou shalt know that I the LORD am thy Saviour,
And thy Redeemer, the Mighty One of Jacob.
For brass I will bring gold, and for iron I will bring silver,
And for wood brass, and for stones iron ;
I will also make thy officers peace,
And thine exactors righteousness.
Violence shall no more be heard in thy land,
Wasting nor destruction within thy borders ;
But thou shalt call thy walls Salvation,
And thy gates Praise.
The sun shall be no more thy light by day ;
Neither for brightness shall the moon give light unto thee :
But the LORD shall be unto thee an everlasting light,
And thy God thy glory.
Thy sun shall no more go down ;
Neither shall thy moon withdraw itself ;
For the LORD shall be thine everlasting light,
And the days of thy mourning shall be ended.

Lesson 74. (Page 154.)

From Isaiah LI; LIII.

HEARKEN to me, ye that follow after righteousness,
Ye that seek the LORD:
For the LORD shall comfort Zion:
He will comfort all her waste places;
{ And he will make her wilderness like Eden:
{ And her desert like the garden of the LORD;
{ Joy and gladness shall be found therein,
{ Thanksgiving, and the voice of melody.
Hearken unto me, my people;
And give ear unto me, O my nation:
For a law shall proceed from me,
And I will make my judgment to rest for a light of the people.
{ My righteousness is near; my salvation is gone forth,
{ And mine arms shall judge the people;
The isles shall wait upon me, and on mine arm shall they trust.
Lift up your eyes to the heavens,
And look upon the earth beneath:
For the heavens shall vanish away like smoke,
{ And the earth shall wax old like a garment,
{ And they that dwell therein shall die in like manner:
But my salvation shall be for ever,
And my righteousness shall not be abolished.
Therefore the redeemed of the LORD shall return,
And come with singing unto Zion;
And everlasting joy shall be upon their head:
{ They shall obtain gladness and joy;
{ And sorrow and mourning shall flee away.
{ I, even I, am he that comforteth you:
{ Who art thou, that thou shouldest be afraid of a man that shall die,
And of the son of man which shall be made as grass;
And forgettest the LORD thy Maker,
That hath stretched forth the heavens, and laid the foundations of the earth.
{ Awake! awake! put on thy strength, O Zion;
{ Put on thy beautiful garments, O Jerusalem, the holy city:
{ For henceforth there shall no more come into thee
{ The uncircumcised and the unclean.

{ How beautiful upon the mountains
{ Are the feet of him that bringeth good tidings, that publisheth peace;
  { *That bringeth good tidings of good, that publisheth salvation;*
  { *That saith unto Zion, Thy God reigneth!*
Thy watchmen shall lift up the voice;
  With the voice together shall they sing:
For they shall see eye to eye,
  When the LORD *shall bring again Zion.*
{ Break forth into joy, sing together,
{ Ye waste places of Jerusalem:
  { *For the* LORD *hath comforted his people,*
  { *He hath redeemed Jerusalem.*
{ The LORD hath made bare his holy arm
{ In the eyes of all the nations;
  { *And all the ends of the earth*
  { *Shall see the salvation of our God.*
For the mountains shall depart,
  And the hills be removed;
But my kindness shall not depart from thee,
  { *Neither shall the covenant of my peace be removed,*
  { *Saith the* LORD *that hath mercy on thee.*
O thou afflicted, tossed with tempest, and not comforted,
  { *Behold, I will lay thy stones with fair colors,*
  { *And lay thy foundations with sapphires.*
And I will make thy windows of agates,
  { *And thy gates of carbuncles,*
  { *And all thy borders of pleasant stones.*
And all thy children shall be taught of the LORD:
  And great shall be the peace of thy children.
No weapon that is formed against thee shall prosper;
  And every tongue that shall rise against thee in judgment thou shalt condemn.
This is the heritage of the servants of the LORD,
  And their righteousness is of me, saith the LORD.

Lesson 75. (Page 156.)

From Job VII.

IS there not an appointed time to man upon earth?
    Are not his days also like the days of an hireling?
As a servant earnestly desireth the shadow,
    And as an hireling looketh for the reward of his work:
So am I made to possess months of vanity,
    And wearisome nights are appointed to me.
{ When I lie down, I say,
{ When shall I arise, and the night be gone?
    And I am full of tossings to and fro unto the dawning of the day.
My days are swifter than a weaver's shuttle,
    And are spent without hope,
O remember that my life is wind:
    Mine eye shall no more see good.
The eye of him that hath seen me shall see me no more:
    Thine eyes are upon me, and I am not.
As the cloud is consumed and vanisheth away:
    So he that goeth down to the grave shall come up no more.
He shall return no more to his house,
    Neither shall his place know him any more.

Job XIV.

MAN that is born of a woman
    Is of few days, and full of trouble.
{ He cometh forth like a flower, and is cut down:
{ He fleeth also as a shadow, and continueth not.
And dost thou open thine eyes upon such an one,
    And bringest me into judgment with thee?
Who can bring a clean thing out of an unclean;
    Not one:
Seeing his days are determined,
    { The number of his months are with thee,
    { Thou hast appointed his bounds that he cannot pass;
Turn from him that he may rest,
    Till he shall accomplish, as an hireling, his day.

{ For there is hope of a tree,
{ If it be cut down, that it will sprout again,
   And that the tender branch thereof will not cease.
Though the root thereof wax old in the earth,
   And the stock thereof die in the ground;
Yet through the scent of water it will bud,
   And bring forth boughs like a plant.
But man dieth, and wasteth away:
   Yea, man giveth up the ghost, and where is he?
As the waters fail from the sea,
   And the flood decayeth and drieth up:
So man lieth down, and riseth not:
{ *Till the heavens be no more, they shall not awake,*
{ *Nor be raised out of their sleep.*
O that thou wouldest hide me in the grave,
  { *That thou wouldest keep me secret, until thy wrath be past,*
  { *That thou wouldest appoint me a set time, and remember me!*
If a man die, shall he live again?
  { *All the days of my appointed time will I wait,*
  { *Till my change come.*
Thou shalt call, and I will answer thee:
   Thou wilt have a desire to the work of thine hands.
For now thou numberest my steps:
   Dost thou not watch over my sin?
My transgression is sealed up in a bag,
   And thou sewest up mine iniquity.
And surely the mountain falling cometh to nought,
   And the rock is removed out of his place.
The waters wear the stones:
  { *Thou washest away the things which grow out of the dust of the earth:*
  { *And thou destroyest the hope of man.*
Thou prevailest for ever against him, and he passeth:
   Thou changest his countenance, and sendest him away.
His sons come to honor, and he knoweth it not:
   And they are brought low, but he perceiveth it not of them.
But his flesh upon him shall have pain,
   And his soul within him shall mourn.

Lesson 76. (Page 158.)

From Ecclesiastes VII; XII.

A GOOD name is better than precious ointment;
    And the day of death than the day of one's birth.
It is better to go to the house of mourning, than to go to the house of feasting:
    For that is the end of all men; and the living will lay it to his heart.
Sorrow is better than laughter:
    For by the sadness of the countenance the heart is made better.
The heart of the wise is in the house of mourning;
    But the heart of fools is in the house of mirth.
Better is the end of a thing than the beginning thereof:
    And the patient in spirit is better than the proud in spirit.
Be not hasty in thy spirit to be angry:
    For anger resteth in the bosom of fools.
Say not thou, What is the cause that the former days were better than these?
    For thou dost not inquire wisely concerning this.
Wisdom is good with an inheritance:
    And by it there is profit to them that see the sun.
For wisdom is a defence, and money is a defence:
    But the excellency of knowledge is, that wisdom giveth life to them that have it.
Consider the work of God:
    For who can make that straight, which he hath made crooked?
In the day of prosperity be joyful,
    But in the day of adversity consider:
God also hath set the one over against the other,
    To the end that man should find nothing after him.
Remember now thy Creator in the days of thy youth,
    { *While the evil days come not, nor the years draw nigh,*
    { *When thou shalt say, I have no pleasure in them;*
While the sun, or the light, or the moon, or the stars, be not darkened,
    Nor the clouds return after the rain:
In the day when the keepers of the house shall tremble,
    And the strong men shall bow themselves,
And the grinders cease because they are few,
    And those that look out of the windows be darkened,
And the doors shall be shut in the streets, when the sound of the grinding is low:
    { *And he shall rise up at the voice of the bird,*
    { *And all the daughters of music shall be brought low;*

Also when they shall be afraid of that which is high,
 And fears shall be in the way,
And the almond tree shall flourish,
 And the grasshopper shall be a burden,
And desire shall fail:
 Because man goeth to his long home, and the mourners go about the streets:
Or ever the silver cord be loosed,
 Or the golden bowl be broken,
Or the pitcher be broken at the fountain,
 Or the wheel broken at the cistern.
Then shall the dust return to the earth as it was:
 And the spirit shall return unto God who gave it.
Let us hear the conclusion of the whole matter:
 Fear God, and keep his commandments: for this is the whole duty of man.
For God shall bring every work into judgment,
 With every secret thing, whether it be good, or whether it be evil.

Lesson 77. (PAGE 159.)

JOB XXVIII.

SURELY there is a vein for the silver,
 And a place for gold where they fine it.
Iron is taken out of the earth,
 And brass is molten out of the stone.
He setteth an end to darkness,
 { *And searcheth out all perfection:*
 { *The stones of darkness, and the shadow of death.*
The flood breaketh out from the inhabitant;
 { *Even the waters forgotten of the foot:*
 { *They are dried up, they are gone away from men.*
As for the earth, out of it cometh bread:
 And under it is turned up as it were fire.
The stones of it are the place of sapphires:
 And it hath dust of gold.
There is a path which no fowl knoweth,
 And which the vulture's eye hath not seen:
The lion's whelps have not trodden it,
 Nor the fierce lion passed by it.

He putteth forth his hand upon the rock ;
> He overturneth the mountains by the roots.

He cutteth out rivers among the rocks ;
> And his eye seeth every precious thing.

He bindeth the floods from overflowing ;
> And the thing that is hid bringeth he forth to light.

But where shall wisdom be found?
> And where is the place of understanding?

Man knoweth not the price thereof;
> Neither is it found in the land of the living.

The depth saith, It is not in me:
> And the sea saith, It is not with me.

It cannot be gotten for gold,
> Neither shall silver be weighed for the price thereof.

It cannot be valued with the gold of Ophir,
> With the precious onyx, or the sapphire.

The gold and the crystal cannot equal it:
> And the exchange of it shall not be for jewels of fine gold.

No mention shall be made of coral, or of pearls
> For the price of wisdom is above rubies.

The topaz of Ethiopia shall not equal it,
> Neither shall it be valued with pure gold.

Whence then cometh wisdom?
> And where is the place of understanding?

Seeing it is hid from the eyes of all living,
> And kept close from the fowls of the air.

Destruction and death say,
> We have heard the fame thereof with our ears.

God understandeth the way thereof,
> And he knoweth the place thereof.

For he looketh to the ends of the earth,
> And seeth under the whole heaven ;

To make the weight for the winds ;
> And he weigheth the waters by measure.

When he made a decree for the rain,
> And a way for the lightning of the thunder :

Then did he see it, and declare it ;
> He prepared it, yea, and searched it out.

{ And unto man he said,
{ Behold, the fear of the Lord, that is wisdom ;
> And to depart from evil is understanding.

Lesson 78. (Page 161.)

From Proverbs III.

TRUST in the Lord with all thine heart;
And lean not unto thine own understanding.
In all thy ways acknowledge him,
And he shall direct thy paths.
Be not wise in thine own eyes:
Fear the Lord, and depart from evil.
It shall be health to thy navel,
And marrow to thy bones.
Honor the Lord with thy substance,
And with the first-fruits of all thine increase:
So shall thy barns be filled with plenty,
And thy presses shall burst out with new wine.
My son, despise not the chastening of the Lord;
Neither be weary of his correction:
For whom the Lord loveth he correcteth;
Even as a father the son in whom he delighteth.
Happy is the man that findeth wisdom,
And the man that getteth understanding.
For the merchandise of it is better than the merchandise of silver,
And the gain thereof than fine gold.
She is more precious than rubies:
And all the things thou canst desire are not to be compared unto her.
Length of days is in her right hand;
And in her left hand riches and honor.
Her ways are ways of pleasantness,
And all her paths are peace.
She is a tree of life to them that lay hold upon her:
And happy is every one that retaineth her.
The Lord by wisdom hath founded the earth;
By understanding hath he established the heavens.
Wisdom is the principal thing; therefore get wisdom:
And with all thy getting get understanding.
Exalt her, and she shall promote thee:
She shall bring thee to honor, when thou dost embrace her.
She shall give to thine head an ornament of grace:
A crown of glory shall she deliver to thee.

Hear, O my son, and receive my sayings;
And the years of thy life shall be many.
I have taught thee in the way of wisdom;
I have led thee in right paths.
When thou goest, thy steps shall not be straitened;
And when thou runnest, thou shalt not stumble.
Take fast hold of instruction; let her not go:
Keep her; for she is thy life.
Enter not into the path of the wicked,
And go not in the way of evil men.
Avoid it, pass not by it,
Turn from it, and pass away.
For they sleep not, except they have done mischief;
And their sleep is taken away, unless they cause some to fall.
For they eat the bread of wickedness,
And drink the wine of violence.
But the path of the just is as the shining light,
That shineth more and more unto the perfect day.
The way of the wicked is as darkness:
They know not at what they stumble.
My son, attend to my words;
Incline thine ear unto my sayings.
Let them not depart from thine eyes;
Keep them in the midst of thine heart.
For they are life unto those that find them,
And health to all their flesh.
Keep thy heart with all diligence;
For out of it are the issues of life.
Put away from thee a froward mouth,
And perverse lips put far from thee.
Let thine eyes look right on,
And let thine eyelids look straight before thee.
Ponder the path of thy feet,
And let all thy ways be established.
Turn not to the right hand nor to the left:
Remove thy foot from evil.

Lesson 79. (Page 163.)

Proverbs VIII.

DOTH not wisdom cry?
And understanding put forth her voice?
She standeth in the top of high places,
By the way in the places of the paths.
She crieth at the gates, at the entry of the city,
At the coming in at the doors.
Unto you, O men, I call;
And my voice is to the sons of man.
O ye simple, understand wisdom:
And ye fools, be ye of an understanding heart.
Hear, for I will speak of excellent things;
And the opening of my lips shall be right things.
For my mouth shall speak truth;
And wickedness is an abomination to my lips.
All the words of my mouth are in righteousness;
There is nothing froward or perverse in them.
They are all plain to him that understandeth,
And right to them that find knowledge.
Receive my instruction, and not silver;
And knowledge rather than choice gold.
For wisdom is better than rubies;
And all the things that may be desired are not to be compared to it.
I wisdom dwell with prudence,
And find out knowledge of witty inventions.
The fear of the LORD is to hate evil:
Pride, and arrogancy, and the evil way, and the froward mouth, do I hate.
Counsel is mine, and sound wisdom:
I am understanding; I have strength.
By me kings reign, and princes decree justice.
By me princes rule, and nobles, even all the judges of the earth.
I love them that love me;
And those that seek me early shall find me.
Riches and honor are with me;
Yea, durable riches and righteousness.
My fruit is better than gold, yea, than fine gold;
And my revenue than choice silver.

I lead in the way of righteousness,
In the midst of the paths of judgment:
That I may cause those that love me to inherit substance;
And I will fill their treasures.
The LORD possessed me in the beginning of his way,
Before his works of old.
I was set up from everlasting,
From the beginning, or ever the earth was.
When there were no depths, I was brought forth;
When there were no fountains abounding with water.
Before the mountains were settled,
Before the hills, was I brought forth.
While as yet he had not made the earth, nor the fields,
Nor the highest part of the dust of the world.
When he prepared the heavens, I was there:
When he set a compass upon the face of the depth:
When he established the clouds above:
When he strengthened the fountains of the deep:
{ When he gave to the sea his decree,
{ That the waters should not pass his commandment;
When he appointed the foundations of the earth:
Then I was by him, as one brought up with him:
And I was daily his delight, rejoicing always before him;
Rejoicing in the habitable part of his earth;
And my delights were with the sons of men.
Now therefore hearken unto me, O ye children:
For blesssed are they that keep my ways.
Hear instruction, and be wise,
And refuse it not.
Blessed is the man that heareth me,
{ *Watching daily at my gates,*
{ *Waiting at the posts of my doors.*
For whoso findeth me findeth life,
And shall obtain favor of the LORD.
But he that sinneth against me wrongeth his own soul:
All they that hate me love death.

Lesson 80. (Page 165.)

From Proverbs XIV.

A SCORNER seeketh wisdom, and findeth it not:
But knowledge is easy unto him that understandeth.
Go from the presence of a foolish man,
When thou perceivest not in him the lips of knowledge.
The wisdom of the prudent is to understand his way:
But the folly of fools is deceit.
Fools make a mock at sin:
But among the righteous there is favor.
The heart knoweth his own bitterness;
And a stranger doth not intermeddle with his joy.
The house of the wicked shall be overthrown:
But the tabernacle of the upright shall flourish.
There is a way which seemeth right unto a man,
But the end thereof are the ways of death.
Even in laughter the heart is sorrowful;
And the end of that mirth is heaviness.
The backslider in heart shall be filled with his own ways;
And a good man shall be satisfied from himself.
The simple believeth every word:
But the prudent man looketh well to his going.
A wise man feareth, and departeth from evil:
But the fool rageth, and is confident.
He that is soon angry dealeth foolishly:
And a man of wicked devices is hated.
The simple inherit folly:
But the prudent are crowned with knowledge.
The evil bow before the good;
And the wicked at the gates of the righteous.
The poor is hated even of his own neighbor:
But the rich hath many friends.
He that despiseth his neighbor sinneth:
But he that hath mercy on the poor, happy is he.
Do they not err that devise evil?
But mercy and truth shall be to them that devise good.
In all labor there is profit:
But the talk of the lips tendeth only to penury.

The crown of the wise is their riches:
> But the foolishness of fools is folly.

A true witness delivereth souls:
> But a deceitful witness speaketh lies.

In the fear of the LORD is strong confidence:
> And his children shall have a place of refuge.

The fear of the LORD is a fountain of life,
> To depart from the snares of death.

In the multitude of people is the king's honor:
> But in the want of people is the destruction of the prince.

He that is slow to wrath is of great understanding:
> But he that is hasty of spirit exalteth folly.

A sound heart is the life of the flesh:
> But envy is the rottenness of the bones.

He that oppresseth the poor reproacheth his Maker:
> But he that honoreth him hath mercy on the poor.

The wicked is driven away in his wickedness:
> But the righteous hath hope in his death.

Wisdom resteth in the heart of him that hath understanding:
> But that which is in the midst of fools is made known.

Righteousness exalteth a nation:
> But sin is a reproach to any people.

The king's favor is toward a wise servant:
> But his wrath is against him that causeth shame.

Lesson 81. (Page 166.)

From Revelation IV; V.

AFTER this I looked, and, behold, a door was opened in heaven:
> And the first voice which I heard was as it were of a trumpet talking with me;

Which said, Come up hither,
> And I will show thee things which must be hereafter.

And immediately I was in the spirit:
> And, behold! a throne was set in heaven, and one sat on the throne.

And he that sat was to look upon like a jasper and a sardine stone;
> And there was a rainbow round about the throne, in sight like unto an emerald.

And round about the throne were four and twenty seats:
> And upon the seats I saw four and twenty elders sitting, clothed in white raiment; and they had on their heads crowns of gold.

And out of the throne proceeded lightnings and thunderings and voices;
> And there were seven lamps of fire burning before the throne, which are the seven Spirits of God.

And before the throne there was a sea of glass like unto crystal:
> And in the midst of the throne, and round about the throne, were four beasts full of eyes before and behind.

And when those beasts give glory and honor and thanks to him that sat on the throne,
> Who liveth for ever and ever,

The four and twenty elders fall down before him that sat on the throne,
> And worship him that liveth for ever and ever, and cast their crowns before the throne,

Saying, Thou art worthy, O Lord, to receive glory and honor and power:
> For thou hast created all things, and for thy pleasure they are and were created.

And I beheld, and, lo, in the midst of the throne and of the four beasts, and in the midst of the elders, stood a Lamb as it had been slain,
> Having seven horns and seven eyes, which are the seven Spirits of God sent forth into all the earth.

And he came and took the book,
> Out of the right hand of him that sat upon the throne.

And when he had taken the book, the four beasts and four and twenty elders fell down before the Lamb,
> Having every one of them harps, and golden vials full of odors, which are the prayers of saints.

And they sung a new song, saying, Thou art worthy to take the book, and to open the seals thereof:
> For thou wast slain, and hast redeemed us to God by thy blood out of every kindred, and tongue, and people, and nation;

And hast made us unto our God kings and priests:
> And we shall reign on the earth.

And I beheld, and I heard the voice of many angels round about the throne and the beasts and the elders:
> And the number of them was ten thousand times ten thousand, and thousands of thousands;

Saying with a loud voice, Worthy is the Lamb that was slain,
> To receive power, and riches, and wisdom, and strength, and honor, and glory, and blessing.

And every creature which is in heaven, and on the earth, and under the earth, and such as are in the sea, and all that are in them, heard I saying, *Blessing, and honor, and glory, and power, be unto him that sitteth upon the throne, and unto the Lamb for ever and ever.*
And the four beasts said, Amen.
And the four and twenty elders fell down and worshipped him that liveth for ever and ever.

Lesson 82. (Page 168.)

From Revelation XIV; XIX.

AND I looked, and, lo, a Lamb stood on the mount Sion,
And with him an hundred forty and four thousand, having his Father's name written in their foreheads.
And I heard a voice from heaven, as the voice of many waters, and as the voice of a great thunder:
And I heard the voice of harpers harping with their harps:
And they sung as it were a new song before the throne, and before the four beasts, and the elders:
And no man could learn that song but the hundred and forty and four thousand, which were redeemed from the earth.
These are they which follow the Lamb whithersoever he goeth.
These were redeemed from among men, being the first-fruits unto God and to the Lamb.
And in their mouth was found no guile:
For they are without fault before the throne of God.
And I saw another angel fly in the midst of heaven, having the everlasting gospel to preach unto them that dwell on the earth,
And to every nation, and kindred, and tongue, and people,
Saying with a loud voice, Fear God, and give glory to him; for the hour of his judgment is come:
And worship him that made heaven, and earth, and the sea, and the fountains of waters.
Here is the patience of the saints:
Here are they that keep the commandments of God, and the faith of Jesus.
And I heard a voice from heaven saying unto me, Write, Blessed are the dead which die in the Lord from henceforth:
Yea, saith the Spirit, that they may rest from their labors; and their works do follow them.

And a voice came out of the throne, saying, Praise our God, all ye his servants,
And ye that fear him, both small and great.
And I heard as it were the voice of a great multitude,
And as the voice of many waters, and as the voice of mighty thunderings, saying, Alleluia: for the Lord God omnipotent reigneth.
Let us be glad and rejoice, and give honor to him:
For the marriage of the Lamb is come, and his wife hath made herself ready.
And to her was granted that she should be arrayed in fine linen, clean and white:
For the fine linen is the righteousness of saints.
And he saith unto me, Write, Blessed are they which are called unto the marriage supper of the Lamb.
And he saith unto me, These are the true sayings of God.
And I saw heaven opened, and behold a white horse;
And he that sat upon him was called Faithful and True, and in righteousness he doth judge and make war.
His eyes were as a flame of fire, and on his head were many crowns;
And he had a name written, that no man knew, but he himself.
And he was clothed with a vesture dipped in blood:
And his name is called The Word of God.
And he hath on his vesture and on his thigh a name written,
King of kings, and LORD *of lords.*

Lesson 83. (PAGE 169.)

FROM REVELATION XXI; XXII.

AND I saw a new heaven and a new earth:
For the first heaven and the first earth were passed away; and there was no more sea.
And I John saw the holy city, new Jerusalem, coming down from God out of heaven,
Prepared as a bride adorned for her husband.
And I heard a great voice out of heaven saying, Behold, the tabernacle of God is with men, and he will dwell with them,
And they shall be his people, and God himself shall be with them, and be their God.

And God shall wipe away all tears from their eyes;
    And there shall be no more death, neither sorrow, nor crying, neither shall there be any more pain: for the former things are passed away.
And he carried me away in the spirit to a great and high mountain,
    And showed me that great city, the holy Jerusalem, descending out of heaven from God,
Having the glory of God: and her light was like unto a stone most precious,
    Even like a jasper stone, clear as crystal;
And had a wall great and high, and had twelve gates, and at the gates twelve angels,
    And names written thereon, which are the names of the twelve tribes of the children of Israel:
And the building of the wall of it was of jasper:
    And the city was pure gold, like unto clear glass.
And the foundations of the wall of the city were garnished
    With all manner of precious stones.
And the twelve gates were twelve pearls; every several gate was of one pearl:
    And the street of the city was pure gold, as it were transparent glass.
And I saw no temple therein:
    For the Lord God Almighty and the Lamb are the temple of it.
And the city had no need of the sun, neither of the moon to shine in it:
    For the glory of God did lighten it, and the Lamb is the light thereof.
And the nations of them which are saved shall walk in the light of it:
    And the kings of the earth do bring their glory and honor into it.
And the gates of it shall not be shut at all by day:
    For there shall be no night there.
{ And they shall bring the glory and honor of the nations into it.
{ And there shall in no wise enter into it any thing that defileth,
    { *Neither whatsoever worketh abomination, or maketh a lie:*
    { *But they which are written in the Lamb's book of life.*
And he showed me a pure river of water of life, clear as crystal,
    Proceeding out of the throne of God and of the Lamb.
In the midst of the street of it, and on either side of the river, was there the tree of life,
    { *Which bare twelve manner of fruits, and yielded her fruit every month:*
    { *And the leaves of the tree were for the healing of the nations.*
And there shall be no more curse:
    But the throne of God and of the Lamb shall be in it; and his servants shall serve him:
And they shall see his face:
    And his name shall be in their foreheads.

And there shall be no night there; and they need no candle, neither light of the sun;
For the Lord God giveth them light: and they shall reign for ever and ever.
Blessed are they that do his commandments, that they may have right to the tree of life,
And may enter in through the gates into the city.
I Jesus have sent mine angel to testify unto you these things in the churches.
I am the root and the offspring of David, and the bright and morning star.
And the Spirit and the Bride say, Come. And let him that heareth say, Come.
And let him that is athirst come. And whosoever will, let him take the water of life freely.
He which testifieth these things saith, Surely I come quickly:
Amen. Even so, come, Lord Jesus.
The grace of our Lord Jesus Christ be with you all.
AMEN.

Index to the Psalter.

	PAGE		PAGE
Psalm I	11	Psalm XLI	91
Psalm II	65	Psalm XLII	16
Psalm III	70	Psalm XLIII	17
Psalm IV	70	Psalm XLIV	93
Psalm V	26	Psalm XLV	63
Psalm VIII	23	Psalm XLVI	17
Psalm IX	86	Psalm XLVII	98
Psalm X	120	Psalm XLVIII	28
Psalm XII	132	Psalm XLIX	95
Psalm XIII	114	Psalm L	97
Psalm XIV	94	Psalm LI	18
Psalm XV	11	Psalm LIII	123
Psalm XVI	23	Psalm LV	111
Psalm XVII	73	Psalm LVI	112
Psalm XVIII (1–35)	71	Psalm LVII	96
Psalm XIX	22	Psalm LIX	121
Psalm XX	71	Psalm LX	133
Psalm XXI	66	Psalm LXI	92
Psalm XXII	124	Psalm LXII	88
Psalm XXIII	24	Psalm LXIII	28
Psalm XXIV	24	Psalm LXIV	87
Psalm XXV	89	Psalm LXV	30
Psalm XXVI	12	Psalm LXVI	31
Psalm XXVII	25	Psalm LXVII	77
Psalm XXVIII	13	Psalm LXVIII	68
Psalm XXIX	51	Psalm LXIX	118 and 126
Psalm XXX	13	Psalm LXX	127
Psalm XXXI	125	Psalm LXXI	106
Psalm XXXII	91	Psalm LXXII	64
Psalm XXXIII	27	Psalm LXXIII	99
Psalm XXXIV	15	Psalm LXXIV	128
Psalm XXXVI	90	Psalm LXXV	78
Psalm XXXVII	75	Psalm LXXVI	78
Psalm XXXIX	105	Psalm LXXVII	79
Psalm XL	115	Psalm LXXVIII	102

INDEX TO THE PSALTER. 173

	PAGE		PAGE
Psalm LXXX	80	Psalm CXXVII	56
Psalm LXXXI	32	Psalm CXXX	19
Psalm LXXXII	94	Psalm CXXXII	55
Psalm LXXXIV	29	Psalm CXXXIII	55
Psalm LXXXV	33	Psalm CXXXIV	55
Psalm LXXXVI	34	Psalm CXXXV	61
Psalm LXXXVII	33	Psalm CXXXVIII	57
Psalm LXXXVIII	117	Psalm CXXXIX	101
Psalm LXXXIX (1-34)	81	Psalm CXLIII	115
Psalm XC	83	Psalm CXLIV	85
Psalm XCI	84	Psalm CXLV	58
Psalm XCII	35	Psalm CXLVI	57
Psalm XCIII	36	Psalm CXLVII	59
Psalm XCIV	129	Psalm CXLVIII	60
Psalm XCV	36	Psalm CXLIX	62
Psalm XCVI	37	Psalm CL	63
Psalm XCVII	38	Exodus XV	134
Psalm XCVIII	38	Numbers XXIII, XXIV	135
Psalm XCIX	39	Deuteronomy XXXIII	132
Psalm C	39	1 Chronicles XVI (8-36)	130
Psalm CI	99	Job VII	156
Psalm CII	113	Job XIV	156
Psalm CIII	20	Job XXVIII	159
Psalm CIV	40	Job XXXVI (26-32)	139
Psalm CV	42	Job XXXVII	139
Psalm CVI	44	Job XXXVIII; XL	141
Psalm CVII	46	Proverbs III	161
Psalm CVIII	48	Proverbs VIII	163
Psalm CX	67	Proverbs XIV	165
Psalm CXI	21	Ecclesiastes VII; XII	158
Psalm CXII	14	Isaiah IX; XII; XXXV	148
Psalm CXIII	51	Isaiah XI (1-9)	143
Psalm CXIV	50	Isaiah XL	150
Psalm CXV	74	Isaiah XLII (1-12)	143
Psalm CXVI	49	Isaiah LI; LIII	154
Psalm CXVII	53	Isaiah LIII; LII (12-15)	146
Psalm CXVIII	52	Isaiah LV (1-13)	145
Psalm CXIX (97-128)	107	Isaiah LX	152
" " (129-160)	100	Isaiah LXI (1-7)	144
Psalm CXXI	53	Habakkuk III	137
Psalm CXXII	54	Revelation IV; V	166
Psalm CXXIII	101	Revelation XIV; XIX	168
Psalm CXXIV	88	Revelation XXI; XXII	169
Psalm CXXV	54		
Psalm CXXVI	16		

www.ingramcontent.com/pod-product-compliance
Lightning Source LLC
Chambersburg PA
CBHW020301170426
43202CB00008B/454